Thomas Cook

Days of God's Right Hand

Our mission tour in Australasia and Ceylon

Thomas Cook

Days of God's Right Hand
Our mission tour in Australasia and Ceylon

ISBN/EAN: 9783337245740

Printed in Europe, USA, Canada, Australia, Japan

Cover: Foto ©Andreas Hilbeck / pixelio.de

More available books at **www.hansebooks.com**

DAYS OF GOD'S RIGHT HAND

DAYS OF
GOD'S RIGHT HAND

OUR MISSION TOUR
IN AUSTRALASIA AND CEYLON

By THOMAS COOK

"Thy right hand, O LORD, is become glorious in power: Thy right hand, O LORD, hath dashed in pieces the enemy. . . . Who is like unto Thee, O LORD, among the gods? Who is like Thee, glorious in holiness, fearful in praises, doing wonders?"

EXODUS xv. 6, 11.

London:
CHARLES H. KELLY
2, CASTLE ST., CITY RD.; AND 66, PATERNOSTER ROW, E.C.
1896

PREFACE

FOLLOWING the example of the Apostle Paul, who "declared particularly what things God had wrought among the Gentiles by his ministry," after his return from his missionary journeyings, I have endeavoured to give in these pages a plain unvarnished account of the remarkable triumphs of the Cross which we were permitted to witness during our recent tour in Australasia and Ceylon. To make sure of impartial and unprejudiced testimony I have inserted reports, as far as I could secure them, written by resident ministers, describing the work in their own churches. This will explain the many personal references the book contains. These would have been omitted, but in most instances they are associated with principles and methods of work which it is important to retain, and the one could not well be excluded without the other.

Ministers have also sent the particulars I give concerning most of the special cases of conversion mentioned in the book. In each case the facts were verified by careful personal investigation. Numbers of enquirers are given, because without figures it is almost impossible to discriminate between one work of God and another. The same indefinite phrases might be used with almost equal appropriateness of a hundred seekers as of a thousand. When it is understood that enquirers are referred to, and not converts, there can be no objection to a judicious representation of such facts. The figures are necessary to a right appreciation of God's work. We are able to form a definite idea of the wonderful manifestation of the Spirit's power at Pentecost, because St. Luke informs us that "the same day there were added unto them about three thousand souls." Our chief aim is to encourage and stimulate the faith of Christian workers.

The physical, geographical, historical, and political elements of the book are chiefly the result of general reading and observation, but information was occasionally supplied by local friends, which I have not hesitated to use.

My use of the plural number includes my wife, who was my companion in travel and toil.

Well do I know how rich our Church already is in such literature as these pages contain, but new stores are required to show that the old spirit and aims survive, and that even in *this* age the gospel hath all its ancient power, and that the wide world over the people respond as readily as ever to "the old, old story" from "the old, old Book."

CONTENTS

CHAP.		PAGE
I.	OUTWARD BOUND	11
II.	WESTERN AUSTRALIA	27
III.	SOUTH AUSTRALIA	41
IV.	SOUTH AUSTRALIA	71
V.	VICTORIA	101
VI.	VICTORIA AND TASMANIA	131
VII.	NEW SOUTH WALES	161
VIII.	NEW ZEALAND	189
IX.	NEW ZEALAND	223
X.	NEW SOUTH WALES	255
XI.	QUEENSLAND	283
XII.	CEYLON	303

LIST OF ILLUSTRATIONS

	PAGE
AUSTRALIAN ABORIGINALS	26
WESLEYAN CHURCH, LECTURE HALL, AND INFANT SCHOOL, PERTH	33
KING WILLIAM STREET, ADELAIDE	45
F. CHAPPLE, ESQ., B.A., B SC.—REV. JAMES HASLAM—SIR JOHN COLTON	51
WESLEY CHURCH, MELBOURNE	100
POST-OFFICE, MELBOURNE	103
REV. A. R. EDGAR—SISTERS OF THE MISSION—MR. DERRICK	107
COLLINS STREET, MELBOURNE	111
REV. SAMUEL KNIGHT—HON. DAVID HAM	142
HOBART FROM THE BAY	147
WAVERLEY WESLEYAN CHURCH	173
SCENES IN MAORI LIFE	188
QUEEN STREET, AUCKLAND	191
MAORI GIRLS	197
REV. C. E. BEECROFT—REV. WILLIAM MORLEY—REV. T. F. PRIOR	222
VIEW OF SYDNEY	257
MR. JOHN CORBETT	275
WESLEYAN CHURCH, BRISBANE	282
DISTRICT SYNOD, COLOMBO	305
CEYLONESE FERNS	315

"But unto every one of us is given grace according to the measure of the gift of Christ. Wherefore He saith, when He ascended up on high, He led captivity captive, and gave gifts unto men. . . . And He gave some, apostles; and some, prophets; *and some*, evangelists; and some, pastors and teachers; for the perfecting of the saints, for the work of the ministry, for the edifying of the Body of Christ."

"The man on whom special evangelistic power is conferred must, as a rule, separate himself from the ordinary duties of the pastorate. He is appointed to other work and must not decline it. His position is one of exceptional honour, and also of exceptional peril. He should be strengthened and sustained by the constant intercessions of the Church."—*Dr Dale's Lectures.*

DAYS OF GOD'S RIGHT HAND

CHAPTER I

OUTWARD BOUND

WHEN the late Mr. Joshua Dawson, of Weardale, was dying, he told certain members of his family that the conviction had grown upon him, during his illness, that I should be sent to the ends of the earth to do the work of an evangelist. This, from such a man, at such a time, coupled with similar impressions of my own, prepared me to respond favourably to the invitation of the South Australian Methodist Conference, which arrived a few months afterwards, to conduct missions under their auspices in various parts of Australia. Not that I believe in following blindly mere impulses. Impressions produced by the Holy Spirit will survive the following tests :—

1. No impression is from God if it would lead us to act contrary to the teaching of the Scriptures.

2. Nor are God-given convictions repugnant to enlightened reason.

3. They harmonise always with our moral intuitions —our sense of right.

4. Impressions of Divine origin come gently, and the more they are prayed about the stronger they become. Other impressions often come with a rush, and fade away when we wait before God to know His will.

5. Outward Providences confirm all inward impressions made on the mind by the Holy Spirit, so shaping events as to facilitate the performance of the duty.

These tests are mentioned, because, often when we have reached "a place where two ways met," they have helped us to discern Divine guidance, and may help others. Certainly in the case of myself and wife, there was a precise adaptation of the Providences of God without, and the intimation of His Spirit within. Regarding both as an expression of God's will, and each as illustrating and interpreting the other, we accepted the invitation of the Australian brethren, and commenced without delay to prepare for the journey. Our one supreme desire was to do the will of God. Every arrangement was made, with the words "If He will" prominently before us; and we wished for nothing else but that His purposes should be accomplished.

The valedictory meetings, held in Exeter Hall, London, a few days before we sailed, filled us with larger hopes, and inspired new courage with which to face the responsibilities of our undertaking. These meetings were organised by the secretaries of the "Out and Out" Band, and attended by representatives from all parts of the country. In the evening the great hall, capable of holding two thousand five hundred people, was filled even to the top gallery. No audience could have been more enthusiastic. Applause was forbidden; but the exuberant feeling was allowed a safety-valve in what our Salvation Army friends would call "a volley." From first to last there was no flagging or diminution of interest. All the speakers spoke words of sympathy and wisdom. Their theme was: "The relation of the baptism of the Spirit to the efficiency of the Christian worker." It was pre-eminently a season of grace and delight, and furnished encouragement afterwards, when we were far away, in times of difficulty and temptation. Before the meeting, the assurance of the Divine presence had been unmistakably given us. His "I am with thee" had chased away all fear, and made the promise of victory sure as though we had seen it. We felt we could praise Him for what He would do, as Jehoshaphat and his people did the day before the victory God had promised them (2 Chron. xx. 17-19). Thomas Champness was right when he said, in speaking of Elijah's triumph over the Baalites: "Many are ready enough to shout when the fire falls; but we want shouters when the stones are selected." We did this at that meeting, staking our reputation and all else on the Divine faithfulness. One quotation from my address will suffice:—

"The promise of victory is as good to us as though the answer were already an accomplished fact. But what is the basis of this confidence? The command: 'Go and disciple all nations,' is preceded by the declaration, 'All power is given unto me in heaven and in earth,' which I take to mean that Christ pledges Himself to make effectual what He sends us to do in His name. He places His infinite resources at our disposal and bids us draw upon Him. If He bids me go as His messenger, with such assurances of His presence and power, He will seal the truth on the hearts and consciences of those to whom He sends me, or His word is a delusion. We know where we are walking when we walk on this ground. We have trodden the path before, and have always found the 'rock beneath' when we have 'stepped out' upon God's written Word. None believe in the adaptation of means to an end more than I do, nor in the prudence that calculates the forces upon which we can depend. My faith is no blind fanaticism, but an intelligent trust. What further calculation is needed when I realise that all power is in Christ and that He is sending me? The command is in itself the promise of ability to perform. Faith is believing that God means what He says, and acting upon it without anxiety about consequences. 'He that believes in Christ does what he cannot do, attempts the impossible and performs it.'"

How abundantly God honoured this confidence, and how He granted the requests of the hundreds who prayed for us, the following pages will explain. At the formation of the Baptist Missionary Society, Mr. Fuller said: "There is a gold mine in India, but it seems as deep as the centre of the earth. Who will explore?" "I will go down," said Mr. Carey; "but remember you must hold the ropes." There is gold in Australia—mines deep and inexhaustible, which have been sadly neglected in the search for less precious treasure. These mines we were asked to help to explore; but many obscure saints at home "held the ropes," whose names will never be known till that hour, when many that are great shall be small, and the small great.

We left London on February 9th, 1894, in the steamship *Oroya*, and had an exceedingly pleasant passage as far as Naples. Calling at Gibraltar we were met by the Rev. W. T. Coppin, our chaplain for the soldiers and sailors stationed there, who gave us a most interesting account of the blessing of God upon his labours, and conducted us over the premises used as a Soldier's Home—the centre of his operations. Many a mother will have cause to thank God for the kindly care and oversight her son in the army received at that institution. It is well that such agencies have become part of our Church organisation. None who visit the place can have any doubt as to the advisability and need of having ministers appointed to this work.

The Oriental appearance of the town, the varieties of colour and of race we saw in the streets, the lovely foliage and flowers, the bright sunshine, and the deep blue sea all around, were most charming. It is almost impossible for those in England to imagine the complete contrast between their own land and this; and to be so near makes it all the more remarkable. As we walked through the galleries of the celebrated rock and saw how strongly it was fortified, we could understand how it has come to be regarded as impregnable.

The Bay of Naples well deserves the praise that has been lavished upon it. It is beautiful alike in outline and in colour, and rich in rare historic memories. Looking from the sea on entering the bay, to the right is Sorrento, the birthplace of Tasso; Pompeii, the city of the dead and the past; Resina, built over the buried Herculaneum; with Vesuvius in the background, outstanding from the rest of the spurs of the Apennines, and fuming away till its vapour cloud is borne fifty miles across the land or the sea. Before you is the city, built like a long, straggling village, rising tier upon tier—a vast amphitheatre—from the magnificent azure waters of the bay, and stretching all along the circular shore, an unbroken range of house-line some ten miles in extent. Crowning the height is the castle fortress of St. Elmo, with its dungeons ninety feet under the ground. To the left the coast is studded with villas and dotted with gardens. There, is the supposed tomb of Virgil; and to the extreme western point, are ruins of old Roman palaces and temples, with the towns Puzzuoli and Baia—the ancient "Liverpool" and "Brighton" of Rome. Behind you, is the island of Capri, beautiful and wonderful, with its memories of the vile Emperor Tiberius, whose ruined palace may still be distinctly seen above the trees.

Naples is the largest city in Italy, and the great centre of social and commercial life. The city proper has a population of five hundred thousand; but in the province, and immediately accessible for our mission work, are at least a million souls. Being Sunday when we were there, we did not join the rest of the passengers in their excursion to Pompeii, but found out the Wesleyan church that we might see something of the Lord's work in the place. We were astonished to find such a handsome and commodious building, erected in one of the most central and densely-populated neighbourhoods. Squalor and dirt abounded, as did the people. To reach the pastor, the Rev. T. W. S. Jones, who lives in the upper storeys of the church building, we had to climb eighty-five steps. From him we received a most cordial welcome, and, of course, a pressing invitation to preach. His importunity was such we could not but yield, and half an hour afterwards we were in the pulpit exhorting a select but earnest English-speaking congregation to do as Caleb did, "follow the Lord fully."

Not a few outsiders came and retired as the service proceeded, their free-and-easy manner contrasting strongly with the decorum to which we are accustomed at home.

Perhaps of all fields of Christian labour Italy is among the most difficult. There, the aid of schools, such as are found so helpful in India, is almost an impossibility. Not only have the workers to battle with the inherent evil of the human heart, but with religious indifference and unbelief engendered by a spurious Christianity. Christianity has been traduced, betrayed, and falsified. We saw enough to realise how much of the Papacy has to be unlearned—its vocabulary, its ideals, and its spirit—before the mind can come to the feet of Jesus and learn of Him. That solid lasting work is being done for the advancement of the Master's kingdom by Mr. Jones and his helpers we have not the slightest doubt.

We took lunch with Mr. and Mrs. Gutteridge, friends from Yorkshire, who have settled in Naples, and have now a large business establishment. They showed us much kindness. Afterwards, Mr. Gutteridge accompanied us to Puzzuoli, where I had promised to preach in the evening. Puzzuoli is the "Puteoli" of the last chapter of the Acts of the Apostles. It was at this very place Paul landed, a prisoner, on his way to Rome, and having found brethren, he tarried seven days. Some of the piers of the mole of this "Liverpool," the then emporium of eastern commerce, and round which the *Castor and Pollux* would sail into the harbour, are still standing; and not far distant the wonderful ruins of the reputed temple of Serapis, and many other relics of the ancient city. The amphitheatre in which Nero watched the games, one of the largest, after the Colosseum in Rome, still gives proof, even in its ruined gallery, of the immensity and magnificence of its proportions — the substructures being intact and fresh, and almost as new, apparently, as in the days of Paul. On the other side of the bay is Baia, before mentioned, the ancient "Brighton" of Rome, of which, among the ruins, only the temple baths still stand, and remains of Cæsar's palace. The earth all around is still covered with traces of past grandeur, which are scattered freely among the olives and fig-trees of the peasant. Not far away lies Lake Avernus, and the descent to the fabled river Styx, and the land peopled by the shades of the dead.

In tombs discovered recently, have been found, between the teeth of the skeletons, pieces of money, placed there to pay the passage of the spirits across the river. Tear-bottles have also been found with the dead, in which friends sealed up the tears they shed at the funeral, that the spirit might know of the grief his departure had caused. (The Psalmist refers to this custom of collecting tears in a bottle in Psalm lvi. 8.) Three such bottles, supposed to be at least two thousand years old, were presented to us, and some very ancient coins, which had been unearthed during excavations in the neighbourhood. One of the coins was in circulation when Joseph and Mary went up to Bethlehem to be taxed at the time when our Lord was born. It bears the image and superscription of Augustus Cæsar, and the date of his reign.

We could not help feeling excited as we stood on such sacred and classic ground. The whole district teems with relics of the past. But to preach amid such associations is something to be remembered, a red-letter day in one's life. Our service was held in the house of Francesco Sciarelli, the oldest of our Italian ministers still living and engaged in the work. An ex-monk of the order of St. Francis, he left his convent to join the volunteers who formed the "holy corps" under Garibaldi, a band of priests.

Having heard Gavazzi preach in the piazza of Naples, he obtained possession of a copy of the New Testament, which was blessed of God in guiding his feet into the way of peace. After his conversion he worked with Mr. Jones in Naples for seven years, and then left for Rome to initiate our work there. It was Sciarelli who, with Gavazzi and Ribetti, stood face to face with the renowned champions of the Papacy, chosen by the Vatican itself, to discuss, in the city of Rome, the question: "Was Peter ever in Rome?" Whatever other result followed the debate, the papist legend of Peter's twenty-five years Pontifical reign was scattered to the winds, and the papal pretension to Pontifical power proved to be an innovation.

Not only had we great pleasure, but liberty and power, in declaring to the congregation at Puzzuoli the good news of salvation and everlasting life. Nor were evidences wanting that the Word was blessed to those who heard.

After service we returned to Naples, and arrived just in time to say a word to the Italians gathered for worship in our church. Mr. Jones interpreted our message, which was to the effect that we had often heard of their faith and love in the Lord Jesus, but to speak to them face to face was a double joy, and to greet them as brethren in the name of those whom we represent in England. After we had wished them God-speed with a few words of Christian counsel, they all stood to thank us, and to request not only an interest in our prayers, but that we would, in their name, salute the churches we should visit during our tour, and assure those of other lands of the interest "they of Italy" take in the progress of the work of God among them.

It was altogether a day to be remembered. We could not but thank God, at its close, for the influences which go forth from our Church there, to regenerate a corrupt society, and revive a purer faith and life amid so much comfortless, soulless unbelief and indifference.

We left Naples on Sunday, February 18th, at midnight, and immediately encountered what the sailors called "rough weather," but which soon developed into a terrible gale. For three days we were "rocked in the cradle of the deep" in a manner we shall not soon forget. For the whole time we were unable to leave our berths. During the storm one of the sailors was much injured, and others more or less shaken. We reached Port Said considerably behind the expected time, but were thankful enough to get there in safety. We stayed about six hours to take on board a fresh supply of coal. This was carried in baskets by a horde of half-clad natives, who looked more like denizens of the lower regions than human beings. As we had heard that the people were a disreputable lot, and that there was but little to be seen in the place, we did not attempt to go ashore.

The sail down the Suez Canal and through the Red Sea was full of interest. We passed where the Israelites are supposed to have crossed on their way to Canaan, and skirted a portion of the desert in which they wandered. It was a fine sight to see the huge flocks of flamingoes, pelicans, and ducks, which abound all along the banks of the canal. Here, also, is almost always visible the mirage which is so inseparably connected with the Eastern desert. Sometimes a reflection of the ship itself seems to be sailing along. When night approached we were still able to continue our journey, as the vessel was provided with an electric projector, which threw the light one thousand three hundred yards ahead. The brilliant light which showed the vessel her way gave us a sight of the banks as we moved along; and a strangely weird picture they presented. The canal cost seventeen million pounds sterling; was begun in 1856 and finished in 1869. Its length is ninety-two miles; its depth, twenty-six feet; the tolls average eight hundred pounds sterling per vessel, or eight shillings per ton of net tonnage. The saving to commerce is five million pounds sterling per annum.

From the Red Sea we had a fine view of the peaks of Sinai, one of which was pointed out as the actual mountain on which Moses received the Law. The intense heat interfered with our comfort before we reached Aden, but after entering the Indian Ocean a pleasant change in temperature was experienced. Tempered by moderate and refreshing trade winds, this new ocean was delightful. Calm as a river, with a clear sky, full of wonderful variety as to shade and colour, with fish and birds, sunsets and moonlight altogether new, we enjoyed it as only those can understand who have had the experience. Each night we had a capital view of the Southern Cross, which was particularly brilliant at the time.

But life on board ship soon became monotonous. How to improve the time was rather a difficult problem. There were too many distractions to read much; and as there were not many passengers of our way of thinking, we did not care to form companionships. Opportunities, however, did occur of speaking for the Master; and these were not neglected.

"I have tried," wrote Norman M'Leod in his diary, "at least for the last twenty-five years, to accept of whatever work is offered me in God's Providence. I have, rightly or wrongly, always believed that a man's work is given to him—that it is floated to one's feet like the infant Moses to Pharaoh's daughter." Our experience illustrated the Divine philosophy of those words. To one who spoke of the impossibility of finding satisfaction in this life, we told of the rest we had found in Christ, and tried to show the way. To another who mourned over a sad bereavement, we spoke of the hope the gospel gives, and urged her to make her calling and election sure. A third asked us if we really believed in a Personal God, to whom we replied: "He is as real a presence to us as you are, we talk to Him as a personal Friend, and the intimacy grows closer and tenderer as the years roll on." These are but examples of the testimony we were able to bear, seed, let us hope, that will germinate unto eternal life.

Colombo, the capital of Ceylon, the land of "spicy breezes," was reached on Tuesday, March 6th. To a newcomer, what he sees there is bewilderingly interesting. When we stepped ashore, we seemed to have entered a new world. The streets teemed with representatives of nearly every Eastern race and costume. Red and yellow were the prevailing colours, and both contrasted well with the dark skins of the people. The gorgeous tints of the flowering trees, the variety and magnificence of the palms, the crotons, ferns, and creepers, with the sweet-scented cinnamon bushes, and the fresh verdure of the grass, combined to form a scene of novelty and beauty unsurpassable. We did certainly appreciate the glimpse our seven hours' stay afforded us of tropical life and vegetation under the most favourable circumstances. But our chief object was to arrange a series of missions for the island, to be held as we returned from Australia. The missionaries heartily welcomed us, and by their kindness contributed much towards the enjoyment of our visit. From the Rev. W. H. Rigby we received much valuable information concerning the work which needed to be done in the strengthening of native

Christians, as well as in the conversion of the heathen. He informed us that, in the opinion of the district Synod, our visit would be as timely as it would be helpful. His convictions as to the possibilities of our missions were most encouraging. The greatness of the need was everywhere apparent.

A run of three thousand one hundred and ninety-seven miles from Colombo brought us in sight of Cape Leeuwin, the south-west point of Australia. From Cape Leeuwin to Albany the distance is one hundred and fifty-eight miles. This was traversed in ten hours, when we found ourselves at our destination, just thirty-six days from the time we left England. We were met, on our arrival, by the Rev. J. A. Jeffreys, who conducted us to the house of Mr. and Mrs. John Robinson, whose hospitality soon made us forget that we were among strangers, and twelve thousand miles from home.

As the mission at Perth, the capital of Western Australia, had been arranged to commence on March 25th, we found we had a week to spare, so we decided to begin at once at Albany. A meeting for Christians was held on the night of our arrival, when many sought the " baptism of fire."

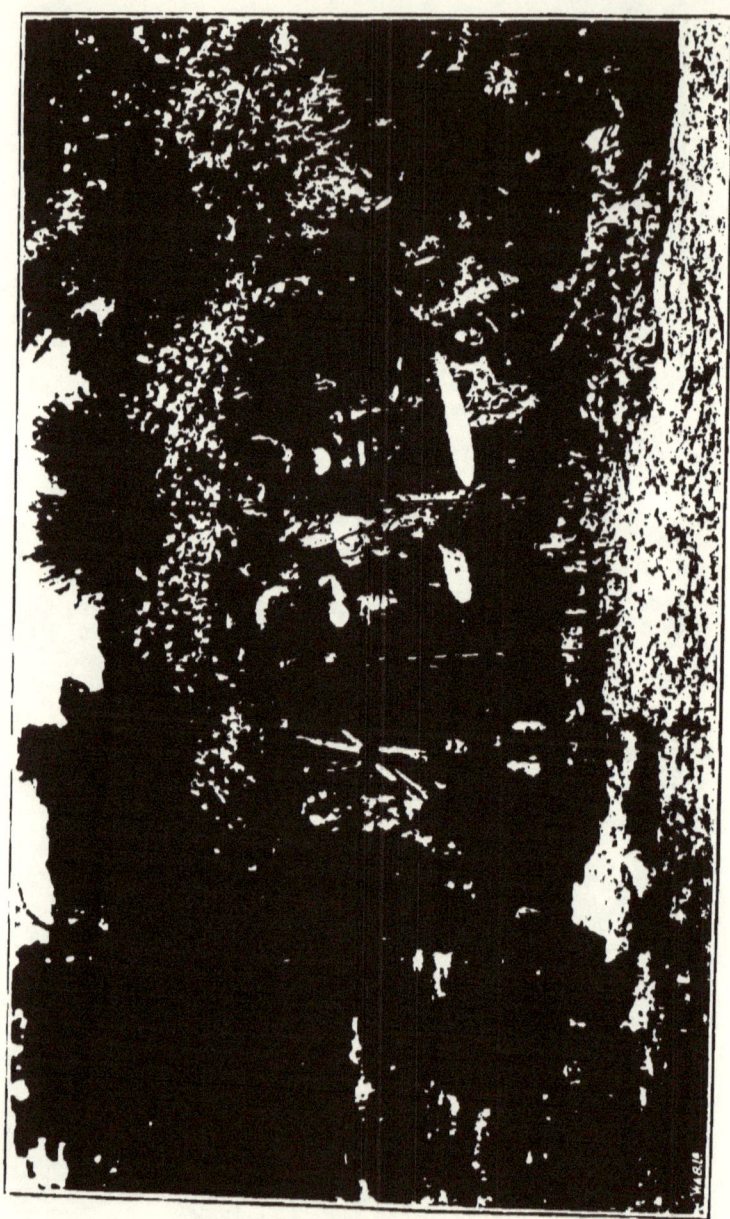

AUSTRALIAN ABORIGINALS.

CHAPTER II

WESTERN AUSTRALIA

Albany—Perth—York

ALBANY is the starting-point for travellers to all parts of Western Australia. It is situated on the shore of King George's Sound, and possesses one of the finest harbours in the world. All mail steamers make it the first and last port of call in going to, and returning from, other parts of Australia. At present the population does not exceed two thousand, but the town is well laid out, and enjoys a temperate and delightful climate, "deliciously cool in summer, and objectionably English in winter."

Our mission commenced with a service to Christians, because we believe a revived Church is the first great need. God will never allow a low type of piety to be widely diffused. In the Acts of the Apostles God's plan for the evangelisation of the world is clearly stated. So long as those lines were followed, the work was done with wonderful rapidity and success. Within one generation paganism was shaken to its centre, and Christianity had spread throughout the known world. The Pentecostal baptism was the grand preparation for the Apostolic Church, and it is still the indispensable condition of success. All filled with the Spirit, and consequently with holy all-absorbing enthusiasm to save the lost, and all "workers together with Him," is the secret of a real and genuine revival. Scripture and history fully establish that this is the Divine method of saving the world. Nothing can be a substitute for the power from on high. No amount of study or talent can take the place of the Holy Spirit. "Until the Spirit be poured out," saints are neither quickened nor sinners saved. "Not by might nor by power, but by my Spirit, saith the Lord."

The time was not lost which we spent in waiting for the Spirit. Many dated from that service new light and power and love. It proved the best possible preparation for the mission. The following day being Sunday, I preached twice, and conducted a service for young people in our beautiful and commodious church, which is capable of accommodating more than half the adult population of the town. At night the building was crowded, and God gave the first-fruits of the glorious harvest He sent us to reap in Australia—the earnest and pledge of grander and more glorious triumphs. Nor was the blessing confined to the unconverted. A letter lies before me from a minister, who was passing through the town and attended the services, in which he says: "I profited much under your ministry on Sunday, and shall look back with devout gratitude and sweet memory to the first service you held in Australia."

Much to our regret, because of the engagement at Perth, we were compelled to leave Albany after four days. Souls had been saved at each service, believers had been quickened and helped, and increased interest and power had been daily manifest. Mr. Jeffreys continued, however, to lead the assault against the strongholds of the enemy with encouraging results.

Perth was reached after nearly twenty-four hours of continuous travel. The journey was long and tedious. We not only stopped at the stations, but wherever we were hailed by passengers who wished to join the train.

The monotony was occasionally relieved by a fine view of the many-coloured bush and wild flowers and beautiful blossoms which enrich the forests of the colony.

Our welcome at Perth was warm and hearty, making us sure that the promise of co-operation would be carried out to the fullest extent. Before describing the work there, let me give some particulars of the colony of which Perth is the capital.

Western Australia was discovered as far back as 1527; but the British flag was not hoisted till 1829. Until recently its progress has been slow, but steady and sure. The fact that, for many years, the country was used as a convict settlement will account, in some measure, for its retarded development. Gigantic strides, however, have been taken during the last three years; and the colony has suddenly emerged into the full glare of the world's light and renown. A zone of gold has been discovered, extending from the extreme north to the extreme south—some two thousand miles, and perhaps four hundred miles wide. This leaves no doubt as to the future of the colony. Men and capital are pouring into it at a tremendous rate, and, in the opinion of experts, the world will hear still more of Western Australia when machinery is more plentiful.

Though including one-third of the entire area of the continent, and covering nearly a million square miles, the population, at the time of our visit, did not exceed ninety thousand. It is difficult to realise the contrast between the vastness of the territory and the sparseness of the population. Were the colony and England peopled proportionately, the former would contain five hundred millions, and the total population of the latter would not exceed three thousand. It is true that since these calculations were made, some thousands have been added to the population of the colony; but, with such an extensive territory, even a hundred thousand would make but little difference. With her boundless pastures, her hills and vales and grassy plains, her forests of timber,—among the finest in the world,—and her stores of gold, copper, lead, and tin, there is room enough in Western Australia for all the surplus population of Europe.

The colony invites settlers. In an interview with Sir John Forest, the premier, he informed me that the government is prepared to offer free grants of one hundred and sixty acres of land to all persons above eighteen years of age who will settle in the country for farming purposes. Let none think that large fortunes are easily made by such settlers. Not many are rich, but scarcely any are poor, and none need be, if they are willing to work. Idlers always return from the colonies sadder and wiser men.

Western Australia possesses, also, one of the healthiest and most agreeable climates in the world. Though it was the beginning of winter when we visited Perth, the weather was exactly like our English summer, and we were informed that the heat of their summer is moderated by sea breezes, which are as regular as they are refreshing.

Perth is pleasantly and picturesquely situated on the banks of the Swan River. The public buildings and streets are far superior to what we expected to find in a town of its size and population. The main street, from east to west, covers a distance of nearly two miles, and is planted with cape-lilac trees, which not only afford grateful shade, but add considerably to the beauty of the place. Nearly all the chief public officials live in Perth, where, owing to the large number of English families which settled in the colony in its early days, English manners and customs are strikingly maintained. To find so little that was new or original was a disappointment. Except that the people are warmer in temperament, more cordial in their manners, and freer from reserve, the Australians are exactly like the stock they have sprung from. Mr. Froude noticed that there was "greater animation of spirits" in Victoria than in England, and the same is true of all the colonies. Their genial climate has much to do with this difference, and their history and training will explain their openness and cordiality.

Perth was unusually active during our visit. The rush for Coolgardie had just commenced, and Perth being the nearest starting-place, hundreds were passing through daily. It was a stirring sight to see the eager faces of the diggers, prospectors, and capitalists, as they crowded the trains which left for this "Bonanza" of the west.

The religious needs of the city are well supplied. For its fifteen thousand inhabitants, there are at least a dozen ministers and as many churches. Our church, which is a handsome Gothic structure, was built to accommodate seven hundred worshippers, but as many more can be crowded into it, as we proved on the second Sabbath of our mission. Large congregations had usually attended on Sunday evenings, but our membership had not increased proportionately. Under the energetic superintendence of the Rev. G. E. Rowe much progress had been made the year before our visit. In all departments the work had been extended, on social lines especially. The establishing of a Sisterhood for visiting and nursing the poor had met with general favour, and had been the means of creating a new interest in Mr. Rowe and his work. This, and much else, contributed to the success of the mission, the time of holding it being most opportune. As no such effort had been made in the city before, we found considerable prejudice and suspicion had to be battled with the first few days. Missions were a new departure; and Australians are no more ready to fall in with what they have not been accustomed to, than English people. It needed some little time, also, to prepare the workers to deal with the enquirers; but the difficulties soon disappeared as the presence and power of God were manifested. The first Sabbath more than twenty adults professed conversion, and before the week ended the first hundred had avowed publicly their decision for Christ. Several of the converts were gold-diggers, who were on their way to Coolgardie. One told us that he had been to the goldfields, and, though not knowing why, he had felt compelled to return. Hearing of the mission, he had attended on the Sabbath, and had been awakened to a

WESLEYAN CHURCH, LECTURE HALL, AND INFANT SCHOOL, PERTH.

sense of his sin and danger. On the following day he realised God's pardoning mercy, and understood then why he had been sent back to Perth.

The crowning day of the mission was the second Sabbath. It was a grand sight to see the church crowded with the sterner sex in the afternoon, and grander still to see them deciding to be on the Lord's side. Two Sinhalese, who had been brought as servants to the colony, were among the seekers. Persons of all classes and conditions of life attended in the evening, from the premier to the dusky aboriginal. All sorts were in the enquiry-room at the close of the service. Not a few were prominent citizens, whose conversion had been long hoped for. It is needless to state that our hearts were full of praise when we learned that fifty-five persons had that day professed to realise Divine forgiveness. The mission concluded on the second Monday, when fifty additional enquirers were reported. The last to enter the enquiry-room was a young man who had been but two years in the colony. In England he had been a class leader and local preacher, but, like many others, when he came among strangers he had not attached himself to any church, and had lapsed into sin. His sighs and groans and tears produced the deepest impression, but they were followed by unspeakable peace. The next day he put into my hand, at the station, the following letter:—

"Good-bye, and God bless you. I only just managed to touch Christ's garment last night. It was almost too late. I was the last to return, and what a struggle I had. I feel if I had left the vestry without settling the matter, I should have lost my opportunity. God help the young men who have given way to infidelity. It is such a struggle to return. For such my poor weak prayers shall always go up to God. Many thanks for your kind help and sympathy."

The spreading flame reached adjacent townships. One minister, who had attended the mission and received a spiritual baptism, told of seven converts under his ministry the next Sabbath. Another re-dedicated himself to God, went to a new Circuit, and commenced his work by holding a ten-days' mission. According to a local paper the result was as follows:—

"The church has been quickened, many having received very special blessing, backsliders have been recovered, while others have been reclaimed from sin and shame. A spirit of hopefulness has sprung up in the hearts of the members. Some are seeking the fulness of the Spirit, others are pressing into the land of perfect love. The minister's hand and heart have been strengthened, and 'still there's more to follow.'"

Our holiness-meetings were largely attended and greatly blessed. Several said those meetings had inaugurated a new era in their religious life.

The two hundred souls God gave us at Perth represent more than will appear at first sight. Taking into consideration the religious condition of the colony, the limited population, and the fact that we were able to remain only nine days in the city, the ministers thought the results were cause for profoundest gratitude to God, and remarkable as exceeding the expectations of the most sanguine. The membership of our own Church was largely augmented, and most of the other churches shared in the benefit. Nearly two years afterwards, when we were returning to England, the Dean of Perth was a passenger on the same vessel. He informed me that several of his flock had been blessed during the mission, and one man particularly, whose life had been altogether transformed since that time.

In a farewell letter, written when we were leaving Australia, Mr. Rowe says: "Your visit to Australia has been immensely blessed to the spiritual good of thousands. I did hope that you would be able to visit Perth again. The Church is prospering on all lines, and 'the best of all is, God is with us.' Your name and work with us are sweet and helpful memories."

We left Perth when the work was just beginning to really impress the town. Nine days were all too short, but other engagements had been made, and could not be altered. Quite a little crowd gathered at the station to see us off, with assurances of kindly interest in our welfare, and promises of remembrance in their prayers. We were not only "loaded with such things as were necessary" for the journey, but with flowers and fruit in abundance. The kindness we received we shall never forget; especially do we cherish grateful memories of Mr. and Mrs. J. P. Walton, whose hospitality we shared. Mr. Walton is chief inspector of schools for the colony. Six years ago he came from Derby to occupy this responsible position. He is now as much respected and esteemed in Perth as he was in Derby before he left.

The journey to the coast was broken at York, where we spent a night; and I preached to a large and attentive congregation, with the result that eight other souls were added to the number of those who believed unto salvation. Two of these had attended the service at Perth on the previous Sabbath, and had been awakened to a sense of their need.

Leaving York at 4.30 the next morning, we drove twenty-two miles through the "Bush" to meet our train at Beverley, which left at 7 A.M. That ride we shall long remember, through magnificent country, with the sun rising in splendour such as cannot be described. We reached Albany late in the evening, to find our steamer had just arrived and would sail at midnight. It was not, however, until 2.30 A.M. that we could get on board and secure our berths, by which time we were so tired, that we were not surprised, when we awoke the next morning, to find we had made considerable progress towards Adelaide, our next sphere of labour. Three days at sea in beautiful weather were much enjoyed, and helped us to recuperate for work in South Australia.

"When we are not living near the throne, our minds become occupied with questions of order, of talent, or of truth; or—if we sink into yet a lower state—with questions of facility, or influence, or wealth. This Church-reform will be followed by great good; the clear development of such a doctrine would bring a revival; more lustre or strength of talent in the ministry would insure progress. We only wait the removal of such and such hindrances to open this door; or we only wait for the supply of pecuniary means and we shall see good done there; or for the accession to the Church of some person of influence, and God's work will prosper yonder. *Faith is sadly wasted when bestowed on such things.* Give them their right value, place them where God has placed them; but the fact that you trust in them shows that your heart is wrong. Wait not for these—for the power is not in them—but for THE BAPTISM OF FIRE."—*The Tongue of Fire.*

CHAPTER III

SOUTH AUSTRALIA

Adelaide—Moonta Mine—Kadina

WE arrived at Adelaide, the capital of South Australia, on Sunday, April 8th, 1894, and were met at the wharf by Mr. John Hill, commissioner of railways, and the Rev. James Haslam. We proceeded at once to the residence of Sir John Colton, with whom we made our home during the first fortnight. A reception and welcome tea was held on the Tuesday, the tea being provided by ladies from the different churches. This was followed by a public meeting in Pirie Street Church, which was largely attended. The Rev. J. B. Stephenson, President of the Conference, took the chair. Representatives of all the churches, except the Anglican, spoke words of welcome. After briefly acknowledging their kindness, I entered directly upon the work I had gone to Australia to do, and urged all present to make a full and complete surrender of themselves to God. The religious heartiness of the service came to us as a pleasant surprise, and the cordiality with which we were received could not have been exceeded. It was the same at every place we visited. One reason was that we had recently come from England, and, with colonists, love for England is a passion. Every Englishman is from "home," it matters not what part of England he comes from. Even the young people, who have never seen the old country, speak of it in terms of affection, and cherish the hope of some day visiting it. A visitor from England revives, among the older people, a thousand tender memories, and seems to bring the homeland nearer. For this reason they all seemed to regard us as personal friends. But we were Methodists as well as English persons, and Methodists are at home with Methodists all the world over. The family name is a passport and an introduction everywhere. Methodism is a spiritual freemasonry, and all who have travelled can tell, as I do, of unexpected and hearty welcomes because they have borne that name. The terms "brother" and "sister" have not lost their meaning among us yet. Besides, was I not a Methodist preacher? Other churches speak of "Our minister," but Methodists say, "Our ministers." As a New Zealand friend put it: "They claim the passage, 'All things are yours, whether Paul, or Apollos, or Cephas.'" On more than one occasion I was introduced as "one of our ministers from England." The Australian Methodists claim all Methodist preachers as belonging to them. For these and other reasons, we were treated with a generosity and affection wherever we went, which could not have been surpassed had we been their nearest relatives. Little crowds gathered at the railway stations when we were starting on a journey; and, not content with this personal expression of friendliness, they would telegraph to friends who lived in towns through which we were to pass, with the result that at almost every important station a little band would be gathered to meet us, bringing flowers and fruit and various other things to minister to our comfort. Among those who met us in this way were not a few who had been blessed in our missions in England. It made my heart thrill to hear them tell how I had been used of God in leading them into His kingdom.

But to return to Adelaide. The city has been happily named "Fair Adelaide," which is a true epithet whether applied to the situation, the climate, or the elegance of its buildings. Travellers are not without reason loud in their praise of the city and the picturesque beauty of its surroundings. It is situated six miles from the sea, on a rising plateau, with a fine range of hills—known as Mount Lofty range—in the background. Park grounds surround the city on all sides, dedicated in perpetuity to the use and recreation of the citizens. These fine open spaces have much to do with the healthiness of the place. The streets are laid out at right angles—the principal thoroughfare, King William Street, is one of the handsomest streets we have ever seen. The buildings are quite equal to those in the best of our provincial cities. The population, including suburbs, numbers about one hundred thousand. For the spiritual needs of the town, churches exist in such abundance that Adelaide has been named "the city of churches." There are no less than thirty-nine Methodist churches, some of which are very handsome and commodious. Our missions were held in two of the largest and most important.

The first—Pirie Street Church—has been designated "the Cathedral of South Australian Methodism" and "the Mother Church." Its erection, in 1850, was a bold and wise step, as it gave to Methodism a status which has ever since been to its advantage. The governor of the colony laid the foundation stone, and its opening marked an era in the history of our Church. Subsequently, galleries were added to meet the needs of the increasing congregation, and there is now sitting accommodation for fourteen hundred people. The adjuncts of the church have been enriched by a capacious lecture hall, vestries, and class-rooms. The entire cost of the property was fifteen thousand pounds sterling. Its commanding and central position was peculiarly adapted for our first mission in the colony. The Rev. Joseph Berry, the present pastor, is a man after our own heart. By his sympathy and hearty co-operation he helped much in securing the results we have to record. Mr. Berry's preaching is characterised by intellectual vigour, moral fibre, and deep spiritual insight—by point, pathos, and power.

Kent Town Church, where we held our second mission, is the most ornate and beautiful of all our churches in South Australia. It was opened in 1865 by Rev. William Taylor, now Bishop Taylor, and recently of Central Africa. The congregation increased so rapidly with the growth of this important suburb, that it became necessary soon to add transepts, the foundation stone of which was laid by Mr. T. G. Waterhouse, whose widow now resides at Hampstead. The church has a seating capacity for eleven hundred persons. The trustees are to be congratulated upon having such a property free of debt.

The Rev. James Haslam is the present minister of the church. He comes from Bolton, in Lancashire

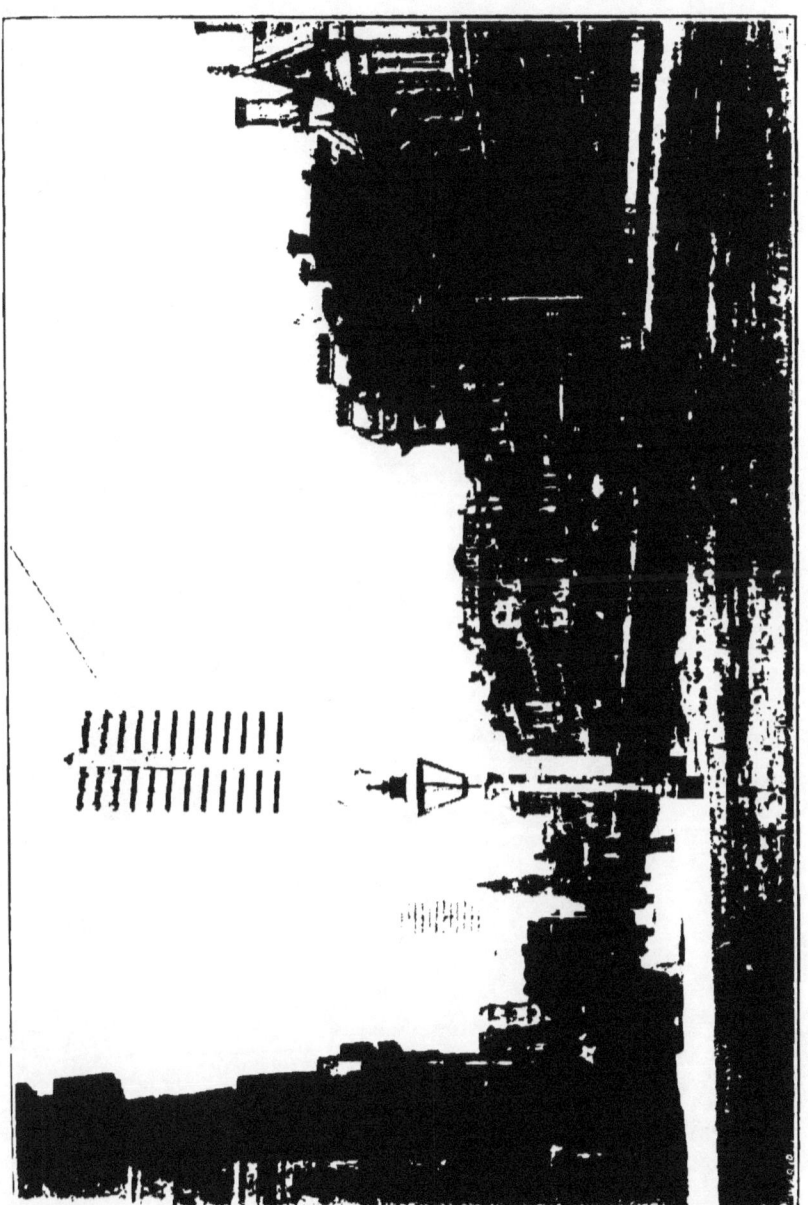

KING WILLIAM STREET, ADELAIDE.

and has done splendid service for the Church in this colony. In 1888 he was elected President of the Conference, and discharged the duties of the office with the marked ability and thoroughness which characterise all his work. He is known as a strong, forceful preacher, and commands attention by the strength of his convictions, and his subdued and devout earnestness. Mr. Haslam was chiefly instrumental in arranging for our visit to Australia, and the manner in which he organised and prepared for us deserves the highest praise.

Towards the success of the Adelaide missions, the courtesy and notices of the press contributed not a little. With some portions of the press of Australia, a man would have a better chance if pugilism rather than piety were his *forte*, but, happily, such is not the case in South Australia. We were literally "boomed" by the leading journals; portraits, interviews, and notices being given almost to extravagance. The result was that congregations, from the beginning, were all that we could desire. A large number of seekers entered the enquiry-rooms the first night, and the mission was launched with every prospect of success.

Night by night the power and interest increased until the Sabbath, when the spacious church was far too small to accommodate the crowds that came to hear. Friday nights were set apart for holiness-meetings, on which occasions the congregations were larger than on any other night. The hunger for instruction on this subject was most inspiring, and the number who received definite blessing was not the least important result of our visit. Conversions multiplied so rapidly, that before the end of the mission between four and five hundred persons had professed to receive remission of sins. Noonday prayer-meetings were largely attended. At these, some remarkable answers to prayer were announced by the workers. Special prayer-lists of at least a dozen names had been recommended; and before the mission ended, the majority of the persons on several lists had found the Saviour. One told of fourteen friends on her list who had been converted. Others rejoiced over seven, eight, nine, and ten, for whom prayer had been answered. At the last service the church was a spectacle never to be forgotten. Looking from the organ loft, a dense mass of faces presented itself, wherever the eye turned, from floor to ceiling. Aisles and passages were crowded, and doorways thronged. But the most interesting sight was that of the new converts, who filled the central area from the communion-rail to the rear of the church, and though two thousand voices made the wall vibrate to the foundations, the song which most affected the ear and the heart was the doxology when sung alone by the four hundred and eighty souls who had been brought to religious decision during the mission. It was a memorable gathering, and one which is not likely to be forgotten, least of all by those for whom it was held. After an address to the converts, a number of others pushed their way into the enquiry-rooms, and so, amid triumph and thanksgiving, closed our first mission in South Australia.

Among the seekers were many of the youths attending Prince Alfred's College. As an educational institution the college dates from 1869; but the memorial stone was laid in 1867 by His Royal Highness Prince Alfred, the Duke of Edinburgh, who had previously consented that the establishment should bear his name. The first headmaster, Mr. S. Fiddian, B.A. of St. John's, Cambridge, left one hundred and three boys on the roll after a two years' term. Mr. J. A. Hartley, B.A., B.Sc., brother of the Rev. Marshall Hartley, succeeded Mr. Fiddian in 1871. Under Mr. Hartley's energetic and able administration the college made such rapid advance, in both efficiency and popularity, that in 1876, when Mr. Hartley retired from his connection with the institution in order to take the responsible position of permanent head of the Education Department in South Australia, there were upwards of two hundred youths in attendance. In April of that year, Mr. F. Chapple, B.A., B.Sc., arrived from England to assume the duties of headmaster, which he has fulfilled ever since. His appointment, from the first, was deemed highly satisfactory, and it has proved throughout eminently suitable. Under his direction and assiduous care, still greater progress has been made. Within five years the students had reached three hundred and twenty-five, and in 1885 it touched four hundred. The college thus acquired the proud position it has never lost, of being the largest and most successful educational establishment of its kind in the southern world.

At the annual speech day in connection with the college, which took place exactly eight months after our mission, Mr. Chapple read his annual report, in which he referred to the work among the boys as follows:—

"There are some subjects which it scarcely seems

reverent to speak of in public, and yet, sir, I should not be doing justice to my own grateful convictions, or to those of my young friends, if I failed to say, that one event will never be forgotten in the records of the year 1894 by me and by them—the visit of the Rev. Thomas Cook. Many before me date from that visit a turning point in their character—a time of decision that will, by God's continual blessing, influence mightily the whole of their future lives."

Our mission at Kent Town commenced, on the Saturday of the same week we finished at Pirie Street, with an address to a large band of selected workers. The enduement of power was urged as the first and ever-continuing necessity for successful service. On the first Sabbath over ninety persons, young and old, decided for Christ. This grand beginning proved that the confidence with which the mission had been looked forward to was not in vain. It was the pledge and earnest of still richer blessing. Every evening during the week brought larger congregations, until the Friday evening, when, at the holiness-meeting, the baptism of the Holy Ghost descended upon a full church. This prepared the way for the second Sabbath's services, which brought blessings above our largest expectations. The afternoon service was for young men, many of whom decided to be on the Lord's side. We had an enormous crowd in the evening, and, what was better, the room was filled with enquirers, who came as soon as they were asked, to seek peace in Jesus. Monday's service was unequalled for impressiveness and results. The constant stream of men and women and young people down the aisles into the enquiry-room led many to ask, "How

REV. JAMES HASLAM.
F. CHAPPLE, ESQ., B.A. B.SC.   SIR JOHN COLTON.

is this? We have never seen it thus before. Truly this is the work of God." Tuesday's service was preceded by a social tea, at which several hundreds of the converts and workers were present. Before my address to the converts, Mr. Haslam asked all to join in praise that we had been sent to Adelaide, and for the wonderful blessing God had given, which he hesitated not to say would raise the whole of the generation with which they would come in contact. In writing to a local paper, he thus describes his impressions of the mission :—

"Whenever our Church's history is written, no previous event will stand out more boldly than that of the mission just closed, during which three hundred and ninety persons have entered the enquiry-rooms as seekers for Christ. . . . An overwhelming thankfulness for such a marvellous reaping is conjoined with a solemn feeling of responsibility. Looking over the list of converts, it is seen that all classes are represented. From halls of the wealthy and cottages of the poor they have come—many young, some old and grey-headed; fathers and mothers who have allowed their children to enter the kingdom of heaven before them, and some who now for the first time see how the most solemn parental responsibilities have been undischarged and unnoticed; children, in whose salvation the prayers of years have found their answer. Husbands and wives that were parted have been made one in the Lord. Many families are now as a whole joined in Christ, and are walking together to heaven. The effect of the mission upon those outside the Church is one of its remarkable features. It is talked of with respect, and with an evidently solemn conviction of its reality. To the Church it has been the occasion of a great uplifting. The converts are identified with many of the churches, and it is scarcely less a matter of rejoicing that the mission has been a stream of blessing, fertilising the other churches, than that it has brought richness to our own. A church consecrated at its opening in the most sacred way,—by the salvation of souls,—in which, in the intervening years, thousands have been saved, and now visited in so marvellous a manner, must surely regard itself as baptized anew to the one great work of every church—the work of saving."

It would be impossible to quote from all the letters received from correspondents whom the mission had benefited. As I write, a great bundle lies before me—all full of joy and gladness—from hearts brimful of gratitude for new-found salvation in Jesus. Those who have borne the burden and heat of the day; men and women who have known better days; young men and maidens, some whose friends are in the "old country"; students, and others from business houses; and not a few parents and children—all join in praising God for the services.

A few extracts will speak for themselves.

A minister from another church writes: "May I be permitted to rejoice with you, and wish you 'Godspeed.' I feel that I owe you a personal debt of gratitude, inasmuch as three of my children, under your guidance, have arrived at the point of decision. You will therefore never pass from our sympathetic and grateful recollection. As his soldiers said of Napoleon, so we say of you, 'He will live in our hearts.' The praises of the congregation are requested by a family of ten, all now united in the service of the Master, six of whom have been converted during the mission."

The Principal of Way College, in sending an invitation to speak at the college, says: "Some of our boys have been impressed at the services, and one of our masters in the Manual Training Department has been converted, and has been bearing witness to the reality of the change."

"Thank the Lord," writes a Sunday-school teacher; "five in my class have come out on the Lord's side this week." Another says: "Nine on my prayer-list have been converted."

"I have been a Christian for twenty-two years," writes a schoolmistress, "and have often sought purity of heart; but I never saw my privilege as at your holiness-meetings. . . . I very tremblingly *took hold*, but I have since felt a peace and tranquillity of soul never realised before. I felt I must tell you what a blessing you have revealed to me."

All the letters tell the same story of salvation found in Jesus, backsliders restored, and believers strengthened and blessed. Among the features of the work was the large proportion of converts belonging to other churches. To no fewer than fifty-nine different churches were lists of converts forwarded after the Adelaide missions. Probably the proportion of Methodist converts did not exceed one-half of the whole. Our object was not to make Methodists but Christians; and this secured for us the confidence of all the evangelical churches. Nor did the work cease with our visit. The flame spread in all directions, as the following letter from a minister will reveal:—

"Your work told with blessed effect on Payneham and Campbelltown. At the latter place conversions have taken place almost without intermission ever since. Though only a small country church, holding about a hundred persons, there must have been between forty and fifty converts—twenty were saved during your mission. At Payneham the taste of soul-saving work was so joyous that I asked my old friend, Rev. John M'Neil, of Melbourne, to give us a week's services, with the result that fifty-five others decided for Christ. We are having conversions—one, two, three, and four—continually at various places in the Circuit. I thought these facts might encourage you."

We left Adelaide with the feeling that God had helped us there as much, perhaps, as He had ever done in our lives. The vast congregations, the sustained and increased interest, the loving spirit of ministers and people, the hundreds of seekers after pardon and sanctification, called for songs of loudest praise. In less than four weeks more than eight hundred persons had entered the enquiry-rooms as seekers of salvation, nearly all of whom professed to find peace with God.

There can be no doubt that our visit to Australia had been well timed. The crash of banks, dearth of employment, and the disappointment occasioned by the disappearance of hard-earned savings had left the people hungering for something more substantial than earthly good. Adversity is a blessing when it leads us to God; and after the commercial disaster, hardship, and suffering they had experienced, we found the people of Australia in a mood to return to Him, and to seek His blessing. Unity and love prevailed also in the churches. Much prayer had been offered and large expectations awakened. Fields were white unto harvest. We had nothing to do but to put in the sickle and reap.

As our method of conducting after-meetings was entirely new, it did not, at first, meet with general approval, though most agreed with us before the mission was over. The usual method adopted was for silent prayer to follow the sermon, then, while the people were quiet and bowed, to plead with them and pray for them alternately. I have found it best to conduct the after-meetings single-handed, and seldom allow any but myself to lead in audible prayer. This is because I have suffered much from injudicious persons engaging in prayer.

Many a church cannot maintain a decent prayer-meeting, because those who ought to pray are usually silent, and certain other men are obliged to occupy the time, whose dreary repetitions become intolerable to all except those who are well seasoned. Such persons have no opportunity of inflicting themselves upon our meetings, and the result is a wonderful relief. Our congregations remain to the after-meetings in a manner which astonishes those who adhere to the old plan of two prayers and a hymn. Then I believe that the man who has just preached has more influence with the congregation while his spell is upon them than any one else could possibly have. It often breaks the continuity of the service to allow another personality to come between the preacher and the people. So I plead alternately with God and the people, until converts begin to move into the enquiry-rooms. Not that this method was invariably adopted. It is best for an evangelist to have no fixed rule in his movements. Some times I asked the awakened to come forward, some times to rise in their seats, and occasionally no movement was called for. Unexpectedness in the conduct of the meeting will not unfrequently surprise the unconverted out of their defences. Where I know the people and *can depend upon them* there is nothing I like better than the old-fashioned prayer-meeting; but such places are few and far between.

From Adelaide we went to Moonta Mine, one of the richest copper mines in the colony. It is situated on York Peninsula, on the eastern shores of Spencer's Gulf, about a hundred and thirty miles from the city. The people at Moonta are almost exclusively Cornish, with all the characteristics of that county strongly developed. Their aversion to new methods, especially the use of the enquiry-room, threatened, at first, to be a difficulty; but the result of the plans we adopted soon disarmed prejudice and established confidence in our success.

After a holiness-meeting, held on the Friday night, reserve broke down completely, and all worked together with a will. Long ago I learned the lesson that if we would convert sinners, we must revive saints. This is not only needful, because the converts in a period of revival are almost certain to conform to the type of the average professor, but because the harbouring of unkind feelings, the want of charity and forbearance, ill-will, the indulgence of prejudices or animosities, prevent the outpouring of God's Spirit, without which all our efforts are vain. The preaching of the doctrine of entire sanctification prepares the way of the Lord by welding together in unity and love

His people as no other truth does. "Indeed," says Wesley, "this I always observe, wherever a work of sanctification breaks out, the whole work of God prospers." Not only does my experience confirm this, but I doubt not that the success of my mission is mainly the result of zealously holding forth this great salvation. Our holiness-meetings were almost invariably turning points in our missions, where previously we had experienced hardness and difficulty. At the service at Moonta not a few purified their hearts by faith, among them one of the ablest and most popular Primitive Methodist ministers of the district. His clear testimony to the cleansing power of the blood of Jesus, at a service I held for ministers the following week, produced a profound impression. On the Sabbath fifty unconverted persons surrendered to Christ; and night by night interest and power increased, until two hundred and seventy persons had avowed their decision to serve God. This result, among a population of between three and four thousand, filled us all with devout gratitude to God. As is usual in Cornish communities, the excitement and emotion of some of the penitents were very great. Their cries and sobs, and their shouts of rapture when the light came, made me live over again experiences in Cornwall, which I treasure among the most precious of my memories. Numerous incidents will long be remembered.

Two daughters who had been converted brought their mother to the Cross. A mother, with her arm round his neck, brought her eldest son, for whom she had long prayed. Two sons went home rejoicing in Christ and asked leave to begin family prayer, with the result that both father and mother were converted. The wife, two daughters, and two sons of a local policeman decided; but he held out. He insists, however, upon the daughters conducting family prayer; and, to his wife's surprise, he knelt himself in prayer before retiring to rest the other night, for the first time in his life to her knowledge.

The after effects at this place were delightful. Thus wrote one of the ministers: "You left us on Saturday, and that evening, at the prayer-meeting, three decided for Christ. On Sunday morning, at 7.30 A.M., I met a class, and found a father there, whose three children you had led to Christ. He had resolved to make a fresh start. That same afternoon, at East Moonta school, a young woman professed conversion; and another at their Monday evening prayer-meeting. We had another seeker at the class-meeting on Friday, the husband of the woman whose sons started family prayer after the Sunday evening service. Then at Mr. Burt's church we had taken turns during the week, with the result, since you left, of over thirty seekers."

Under date June 13, he writes again:—

"Souls are being saved every night, and the interest is growing rather than abating. We must have had over two hundred seekers since you left. After a fortnight with the Primitive Methodists, we went for ten days to the Bible Christian Church. The result being ninety-one enquirers; while at Cross Roads, in three nights, there were seventy others. Every ordinary service produces good results also.

"Yesterday, I was sent for to baptize a child belonging to a woman who was staying with her mother from Port Pirie. While I was at the house, the post came in with a letter for the child's mother. She opened it listlessly, but soon commenced to jump and shout, 'My George is converted! O praise the Lord, my husband is saved! He was converted at Mr. Cook's mission last night.'"

Our third letter is from the Rev. A. P. Burgess to his father at Adelaide, and was published by him in the Methodist paper, *The Christian Weekly*. It reports still further progess.

"The work of God is unabated, and souls are coming to Christ every night. Services are being held at Moonta Mines, Cross Roads, and Moonta continuously, and for all practical purposes Methodist union is a reality; while at every service souls are being born into the Kingdom. Last Wednesday night, while you were all saying farewell to Mr. Cook, forty precious souls knelt at the penitent form in connection with our united services at Moonta alone, while Mr. Burt reports conversions every night at the Mines. On Sunday, in six different churches that I know of, including every church on the Mines, sinners came to Christ. This does not include Cross Roads, of which I have not heard. Since Mr. Cook came here I can account for seven hundred and eighty-nine, but there must be a good number more, as many are deciding for Christ at home, and in our class-meetings and prayer-meetings also. To God be all the glory. A large singing-party from the Mines visited Moonta last night, and made the town ring with the songs of Zion. Men are doing their work here to the tune of 'Eglon,' and the grand old hymn, 'Rock of Ages' is to be continually heard, sung as only Cornishmen can sing. There is every sign of the good work continuing. We are all very tired, but very, very happy."

About the same time Mr. Burgess wrote to me. The letter is dated two months after our mission. It contains most cheering information: "The work goes on apace. . . . Last Wednesday we had forty-one precious souls at the penitent form. . . . On Sunday there were conversions in six of the churches that I know of. Last night made the fifty-seventh consecutive night in which we have seen souls saved. I have not missed a meeting. . . . Moonta has never had such a revival in its history. It has seen larger numbers, but so many old people going to the penitent form is unheard of, and that is the common thing now. Of the first hundred seekers at our last mission all were over fifteen years of age except one.

"The following is the list since the work commenced:—

"Rev. Thomas Cook's Mission, May 9th to 18th . . 278
United Services, Moonta Mines, Primitive Church . 51
United Services, Moonta Mines, Bible Christian Church 136
Primitives, Moonta 21
Bible Christians, Moonta 102
Wesleyans, Yelta 34
Cross Roads 150
Ordinary Services 28
                                                    ———
                                                    800"

Mr. Burgess concludes by stating that he has not been able to obtain the number of those converted at home, nor under the labours of the local preachers and Salvation Army.

The angel of requests—so the legend runs—goes

back from earth heavily laden every time he comes to gather up the prayers of men. But the angel of thanksgiving, of gratitude, has almost empty hands as he returns from his errands in this world. But this was not true of Moonta. They held a thanksgiving service, which was properly described by a local paper as a " notable " one. The following sketch will be read with interest :—

"A united thanksgiving service was held in the Moonta Mines Wesleyan Church on Monday, July 23rd. The evangelistic services having been of an inter-denominational character, it was only fitting and right that the public act of thanksgiving should be of the same nature. The night was dark and the roads muddy, but the enthusiastic endeavourers of the township formed a long procession, and, picking their way through the slush and mud by the light of several torches, came singing through the streets. Another singing band left East Moonta, and met the first near Mines' offices ; a contingent of the Mines' Endeavour Societies being also present. The united party sang up Wesleyan Street to the church, arriving a little late to find between eight and nine hundred people present. It would be difficult to describe the meeting. Seven short addresses were given by the four ministers and three senior Circuit stewards ; the church choirs all amalgamated. We noticed members of six different churches helping to lead the singing; it was a foretaste of Methodist union and heaven—some think the former term includes the later. The Yelta friends were absent. On Sunday night three young men sought and found the Saviour at Yelta, and they stopped away, holding a service in their own church for the sake of other anxious ones. The Rev. J. D. Langsford took the chair, and compared the present revival with the great one of nineteen years ago, quoting from the local papers. The Rev. A. P. Burgess, who followed, mentioned that nine hundred and seven had professed to find peace with God in the different churches during the ten weeks since May 9th, beside which a number had decided for Christ in their homes and at their work. Mr. Cornelius, the Circuit steward of the Primitive Methodist

Church, spoke on the power of church fellowship, urging all new converts to join a church. Mr. Adams led the congregation in a solemn act of thanksgiving, and the doxology was sung. The Rev. O. Lake had been present at the revival nineteen years ago, and in comparing the two a most noticeable feature was the prevalence to-day of a spirit of unity, all sections of the community uniting with one aim and one purpose. Mr. Symons, the Circuit steward of the Bible Christian Church, spoke on work and its power to keep interest quickened and alive, urging every new convert to start and lead another to Christ. The Rev. J. Burt drew attention to the fact that in several centres the interest was unabated, and called for sustained efforts on the part of all. The singing between each speech went with a swing, and was a feature of the evening. A collection was taken up and divided between each church for the benefit of the poor. The influence of the gathering was most inspiring. To God be all the glory."

The next place visited was Kadina, another small town, with a population similar to Moonta, and about ten miles distant. The news of the work at Moonta had preceded us, and had created considerable expectation. We found a hearty and united people. Our first convert was a young lady who was awakened and saved on the Sunday morning. Contrary to custom I was led, that morning, to preach more directly to the unconverted. It seems she had determined not to attend any of the services, and was present on that occasion only, because she expected the sermon would be for those who were already Christians. At the close of the service she came forward in deep distress, and said the message had all been for her. Before she left she was filled with joy and peace through believing in Jesus, and afterwards became one of our best workers.

The first Sabbath the number of seekers was not large, but each night afterwards we had thirty-six in the enquiry-rooms. The coincidence in the number each evening caused such general interest that, among the workmen of the smelting works, the question was asked each morning, if the number had been maintained. Even unconverted men would ask if they had had the "thirty-six" the night before. The Rev. Isaiah Perry has since sent me particulars of some of the converts, which show that we gathered of every kind,

(*a*) A man; thirty-six years years of age. Seventeen years ago he was a local preacher, and twelve years ago a probationer for the ministry. He was a married man, and domestic trouble caused his fall. He and his wife both re-dedicated themselves to God. He determines to work for Christ, but grieves over lost opportunities. Said he, "I was almost lost, but, thank God, He has saved me; the worst is that the opportunity for service has gone."

(*b*) A man; forty-three years of age. The previous Monday he was before the local police court, and fined for being drunk and disorderly. He and his wife both give evidence of a real change. His conversion occasioned wonder, and created confidence.

(*c*) A well-educated young man; whose parents are Presbyterians. He had been the cause of considerable anxiety to his family. A week before his conversion, a brother from Sydney had written to say that he believed George would soon be saved. This impression had come to him while engaged in prayer. The young man seems fully determined to follow Christ.

(*d*) A backslider for twenty years. The memory of the past haunted him, especially the neglect of a widowed mother in England. While seeking the

Lord he exclaimed, "Oh, the burden of the past!" He is now an earnest worker. His wife and daughter have since been saved.

(*e*) A woman; who was converted in her own home while working at her sewing-machine. Leaving her work she hastened to tell her joy to a neighbour with whom she had previously quarrelled, and besought her forgiveness.

(*f*) A man; forty-seven years of age, who has passed through many Cornish revivals, but without conversion. In this, however, he has been "knocked over," as he terms it, and is determined to try and make up for lost time.

With this list is enclosed a letter and resolution from the Quarterly Meeting of the Kadina and Wallaroo Circuit. The resolution reads as follows:—

"This meeting expresses its devout gratitude to Almighty God for the great success which has attended the visit of Rev. Thomas Cook to this Circuit. The mission has been blessed of God to the spiritual quickening of our people, and the ingathering of many persons, both young and old; while other churches have participated largely in the success. This meeting earnestly prays that the good work which has been commenced may continue, and that the Divine blessing may still rest upon the labours of His servant."

In the letter, Mr. Perry tells of the progress of the work. "We had a social tea for the converts on Monday night. About two hundred were present, and a fine sight it was. Everybody was exceptionally happy, and altogether the gathering was a great success. Many direct answers to prayers have been received.

Homes have been completely transformed, and the social and religious aspect of the people quite changed. We have had, already, over three hundred cases of decision for Christ."

The mission filled the hearts of all Christian people with thankfulness, and prompted them to seek and expect conversions more than they had ever done before. At Moonta and Kadina the churches were wise enough to work while God worked. Some ministers have special gifts to teach, others to incite; one prepares the fuel and the other kindles it. But when it is kindled, let the churches know that their opportunity has come and bestir themselves to carry on the work. No help from outside is useful which tends to release ministers and people from a full sense of personal responsibility. If the impression prevails that the visit of the evangelist relieves those on the spot from obligation, no real good can result. The mission should be only the beginning of a continual adding unto the Lord. And to allow the work of conversion to cease with the departure of the missioner is as wrong as it is unwise.

"Lord, give me every year
More burning zeal for souls immortal!
Make me plead with such with earnestness intense,
Love strong as death, and faith God-given.

Will the world cry 'Mad'?
I would be mad—such madness be my joy!
For thrice it blesses: first, my own cold heart;
Then glorifies my God; and plucks, perchance,
My sin-stained brother from the jaws of death."—*Anon.*

Brainerd had such a burning earnestness that he said: "I cared not where or how I lived, or what hardships I went through, so that I could gain souls for Christ." Henry Martyn was another such flame of fire; his earnestness beamed from his countenance, and spread itself among men; his very portrait seemed inspiring. Charles Simeon had it hanging against the wall, and he said it seemed to say to his very soul: "Be in earnest, don't trifle, don't trifle." And Mr. Simeon would reply: "Yes, I will be in earnest; I won't trifle, souls are perishing." The weeping of John Welsh during the night would some times awaken his wife, and when she asked why he wept he would say: "I have the souls of three thousand persons to answer for, and I don't know how it is with many of them." Such are the men God uses—men whose souls throb with Divine sympathies, and who say, as Paul did: "This one thing I do."

CHAPTER IV

SOUTH AUSTRALIA

Kooringa—Port Pirie—Broken Hill

IT was while we laboured in Moonta that the Triennial or General Conference met in Adelaide. Australasian Methodism is governed by five Annual Conferences, held simultaneously in New South Wales, Victoria, South Australia, Queensland, and New Zealand, whose functions are purely administrative; with a Triennial Conference whose powers are exclusively legislative. The General Conference consists of ministers and laymen in equal numbers, who are sent as representatives from the Annual Conferences. The brethren assembled at Adelaide sent me an invitation to address the Conference, with assurances of an affectionate welcome to their shores. In reply I thanked them for their hearty greeting and good wishes, but asked to be excused the speech. Some wrote expressing disappointment that I had not complied with their request; but had I done so the mission at Moonta would have suffered; and it is more congenial to me, to do the work than to talk about it; I therefore remained at Moonta with the results already described. The following returns represent the territory under the jurisdiction of the

General Conference:—Ministers, 645; Local Preachers, 5231; Churches, 2717; Other Preaching Places, 2002; Church Members, 93,274; Colleges, 11; Sunday-school Teachers, 17,647; Sunday-school Scholars, 177,517; Adherents, 455,871.

Dr. Dale said, after visiting the colonies: "Methodism has shown magnificent vigour," and, in the light of these statistics, the testimony is true. "There is something," he continued, "in the organisation, creed, characteristic spirit of Methodism that makes it a great religious force in a British colony." Not only have we held our own, but our Church has grown every year to a position of greater strength in relation to the population of the colonies. Already one-tenth of the entire community belongs to us. Religious equality and freedom, which exist everywhere, will, in some measure, account for this success. With no State-church exclusiveness to contend against, we have had opportunities such as are not possessed in England. Besides, the Episcopalian Church in Australia is, in most places, so "high" that it repels some of their best and most devoted people, many of whom worship with us. In connection with his diocesan visitations, one bishop, at least, had a dance given in his honour at almost every place he visited. Catering to worldly tastes, which often means a letting down of the high standard of New Testament piety, does not fill the churches, nor does resort to human expedients or devices. When we were in Australia, the papers were discussing the question: "Why do not men go to church?" Some suggested a prior question: "Is it really true that men do not go to church?" One editor undertook to find an answer to the latter query. He sent men to count at the chief places of worship. The report was worth more than a thousand letters. At the Salvation Army barracks men were in the majority. At the Presbyterian church the sexes were about equal. There entered into the Wesleyan church just five more women than men. At St. Michael's (Anglican), the figures showed ninety-six men and a hundred and seventeen women. At the cathedral, where the service is "very high," the rate was about two women to one man. The figures go to prove that the "higher" the service, the fewer the men. In explaining the reason for the difference between "high" and "low," one paper suggested that the subordination of the sermon was the cause; but I think, with the editor of our Methodist paper, "a manly dislike to what Froude calls 'the magical theory of the priesthood' has more to do with it." The Dean of Norwich recently spoke of churches of "incense and nonsense" as denuded of men.

We formed the highest estimate of the ability, zeal, and devotion of the Australian ministers. Having travelled that Methodist Canaan, from Dan to Beersheba, we know them well, and the sort of stuff they are made of. As they do most of the entertaining, we often shared their hospitality, and now desire to make grateful acknowledgment of all the kindness, forbearance, and goodwill, which were uniformly extended to us by the brethren with whom we came in contact, as well as the genial welcomes with which they everywhere greeted us during our travels. Spiritually and mentally, they are at least equal to the average minister at home. Many have been trained in our English institutions, others are natives, or colonial born. Speaking of natives, one of our English Methodist papers, some years ago, congratulated the Australian brethren on the fact that out of nine candidates for the ministry, five were aboriginals —just as it should be, the editor thought. He, poor fellow, did not discriminate between natives and aboriginals; but the Australians felt sorry for him that he did not know better. Aboriginals are the low and degraded people who inhabited the continent when the British took possession in 1770. There are but very few of these left, and attempts to Christianise them have met with very moderate success. It is difficult for men born in England to adapt themselves to the rough-and-ready life some ministers have to live in the "Bush" Circuits; consequently the "native" does quite as well for all purposes as the Englishman, and perhaps a little better.

Nothing is more wonderful than the love and sympathy which bind the brethren together; and I take leave to believe that there is no grander brotherhood in the world than that of the Methodist ministry. Many in Australia know much more about what is going on in England than those who live in this country. The questions they asked me about the ministers at home were as interesting as they were varied. Though they have never seen each other in the flesh, they rejoice in mental pictures and spiritual introductions which others give them. In all our doings they take the liveliest interest, and copy all that is best in our methods of work.

We thought the pastoral element predominated in the Australian ministry somewhat to the neglect of the evangelistic. Ministers preach oftener to the same congregations, and seem to lose the forceful manner of appeal so essential to soul-saving. The art of soul-saving must be cultivated, or the gift will be lost; and many lose it by allowing other considerations to become paramount. It is true that all men do not, in the same measure, possess the evangelistic gift. Gifts vary. " There are diversities of gifts but the same Spirit." Nor does evangelistic or converting power necessarily imply superior piety. Results are modified by temperament, mental constitution, and spiritual capacity. All men are not constitutionally endowed with that peculiar, persuasive, and commanding power which successful soul-winners possess. " God does not allow some to become reapers because they do the ploughing so well." Some prepare the soil and others reap the harvest, but many might be reapers who are not, if they would give themselves more directly to soul-saving work. Father Watsford, W. G. Taylor, Rainsford Bavin, and others are doing noble service in helping the Australian ministers to gather in the fruit of their labours, but where they have one man with the evangelistic gift, they seem to have a hundred " pastors and teachers." This will explain why the membership in Australia is so much smaller in proportion to the congregations than it is in England. In England every pond seems to have been well fished, but yonder the unconverted abound in the churches. We found hundreds ready and waiting to be helped into the Kingdom, which will enable our readers to understand how it was that the work of ingathering commenced, at each place we visited, almost immediately we arrived.

Kooringa, the next place visited after Kadina, was no exception to this rule. During the five days we were able to give them, no fewer than one hundred and sixty persons professed conversion. It was at this place that the famous Burra Burra copper mine was discovered in 1845; but during the last fifteen years it has not been worked, owing to the low price of copper, and the fact that the mine had become exhausted of its best deposits. The closing of the mine greatly reduced the population, which does not now exceed fifteen hundred. The country all around is used for pastoral purposes. Immense flocks of sheep are reared in the neighbourhood. As many as a hundred thousand are owned by one farmer. Our congregations consisted of persons from all parts of the district within fifty miles. The church, which will accommodate five hundred worshippers, was inconveniently crowded the first Sabbath, and that day we rejoiced over more than fifty seekers.

At the last service we witnessed a scene, which those who were present will never forget. A band of young men, about thirty strong, had attended all the services. Particular interest was centred in them, because many belonged to our own families, and others had been trained in the Sunday school. Much prayer had been offered that they might be won for Christ; and the last night of the mission had come with scarcely any break in their ranks. After the sermon we noticed how deeply serious many were; but none would yield to our appeals. The after-meeting was far advanced, and some had begun to fear that they had hoped in vain, when one noble fellow stood up in the midst of his companions, and, with the eyes of the whole congregation upon him, walked deliberately down the gallery steps, along the aisle of the church, and into the enquiry-room. Such decision had immediate effect upon the others. A second soon followed, then another and another, until quite a score had come, broken down and penitent, to confess decision for Christ. As they walked down the aisle, one by one, each manifestly acting for himself, because no two came together, parents and friends clapped their hands and shouted for joy. Some wept and praised God aloud, and all said: "It is the Lord's doing, and it is marvellous in our eyes." More than forty persons professed to receive remission of sins in that service, and amid flowing tears and resounding praises we parted, pledging ourselves to meet again beyond the river.

One of our best workers at Kooringa was Dr. Brummitt, a greatly-beloved physician. He called to tell us, one morning, that his two sons had been converted, during our Kent Town mission, and that during the mission at Kooringa, his two servants, his coachman, and charwoman had all been brought to God. He also said: "I have loved you, Mr. Cook, for some years now, because of the help you rendered to a medical friend of mine in the old country. We were students together, and I had the joy of leading him to the Saviour. He became a devoted Christian and my bosom companion. We had sweet fellowship in the Master's service until he went to England to complete his studies. He became assistant to a London practitioner who was an atheist; and while in his house, he was robbed of his faith. This led to his going altogether wrong, and such misery followed that he decided to return to Australia. Before doing so he went to visit my mother, and on the Sabbath she took him with her to the Methodist chapel. It so happened that you were conducting a mission in that chapel at the time, and your message reached his heart. It brought back old memories, and led him to seek again the blessedness he had lost. Nor did he seek in vain. Before he left my mother's home he had restored to him the joy of God's salvation. All this he wrote and told me a week or two before he sailed, but he never reached Australia, he died on the voyage and was buried at sea. I have often longed to see you and tell you all this, but never thought I should. Now, I have to thank you, because you helped me when you helped my friend."

We finished at Kooringa the first day in June, and in November received the following communication, signed by the secretary of the Christian Endeavour:—

"At our Christian Endeavour Half-yearly Meeting, held a short time since, humble gratitude was expressed for God's blessing on your mission in Kooringa. Since your visit our society has been greatly strengthened by new members, and the older ones revived. The Saturday night prayer-meeting, which was started during your mission here, has also been vigorously kept going by the young converts, and has proved a constant blessing to them. A resolution was passed in our Society that you should be informed of the warm regard our young people still have for you, and we hope to prove in the future that your labours among us were not in vain. It filled our hearts with a deep holy joy that we were honoured of God with the privilege of being associated with such work, especially in view of its far-reaching possibilities. Daniel Webster's words were often in our minds : 'If we work upon marble, it will perish ; if we work upon brass, time will efface it ; if we rear temples, they will crumble into dust; but if we work upon immortal minds, if we imbue them with principles, with the just fear of God, and love of our fellow-men, we engrave on those tablets something that will brighten to all eternity.'"

Two days after finishing at Kooringa found us started at Port Pirie. The town, which has a population of about four thousand, is situated, like Moonta, on the eastern shore of Spencer's Gulf. It is the port for Broken Hill silver mines ; and upon the prosperity of the mines its trade largely depends. Extensive smelting and refining works furnish employment for a large number of men. These preponderated in our services, and many were converted. Because our church was not sufficiently commodious to accommodate the crowds we expected, the Institute Hall was engaged for the mission. It was not well suited for such services, but we were obliged to make the best of what we had. To make provision for enquirers was one of the chief difficulties. Some suggested that we should use the dressing-room at the back of the stage, but the room would not accommodate more than a dozen, so I asked what would be done when fifty came. They had not dreamt of such a number at any one service ; but I insisted that that number should be provided for. This meant clearing out an old lumber-room which was full of stage properties and other rubbish. So, taking off my coat, I said, " Gentlemen, let us get to work." In three hours the place was entirely transformed. The earthen floor was covered with boards, over which we spread carpets; the holes in the sides of the building were covered with tarpaulin; boxes and battens were utilised for seats, and all was ready. The news spread like wildfire of what we had done, and brought the people in such crowds the following day, that the building—which would seat seven hundred persons—proved too small for the occasion, and afterwards scores had to be often turned away who could not be accommodated. At first the forces of evil leagued themselves to oppose. Certain scoffers indulged in a parody of our proceedings at an adjacent public-house. But the raging of the adversary was only the prelude to extraordinary blessing. Under the mighty operation of the Spirit of God, a strange fear came upon the town, until men who were far from being religious, confessed that they had never known the people so impressed before. Religion became the chief topic of conversation, and all spoke of it with profound respect. The pastor himself, the Rev. Thomas A. James, shall describe the mission:—

"Great expectations were aroused in the hearts of the Christian people of Port Pirie, when it was known that the Rev. Thomas Cook was coming to conduct a ten-days' mission. Signs of revival had been gathering for some time. It was confidently believed that the day of visitation had come, and God's people were ceaseless in prayer. The Institute Hall was hired for the mission, as it was the only building in the town at all adequate to accommodate the numbers who were expected to attend. On Sunday, June 3rd, the mission began with a prayer-meeting at 7 A.M., when, in spite of the dark, damp morning, nearly one hundred persons assembled. It rained heavily before the morning service, but hundreds found their way to the hall. On Sunday afternoon there was a service for young people; rain overhead and slush below did not prevent the hall from being well filled. Mr. Cook spoke to the young people on the importance of decision for Christ, and, in response to his appeal, thirty pressed into the enquiry-room. More rain, but a full hall at night, and many decisions for God. The mission was now fairly launched; and neither wet weather, bad roads, nor long distances prevented the people from attending. Night after night the interest deepened, until the whole town was roused. The congregations that assembled were unprecedented in the history of Port Pirie. All classes and creeds were represented, and people came from near and from far. One prominent feature of the mission was the large attendance of men at the services. Every night the Word was preached with demonstration of the Spirit and with power. The holiness-meeting of Friday evening was a memorable time. Mr. Cook's exposition of the great privilege of believers to enter into the holiest by the blood of Jesus, and to claim 'the continual cleansing from all sin,' was very helpful. God's people were blessed unspeakably, and between forty and fifty persons entered the enquiry-room to seek and to find pardon of sin. The second Sunday of the mission began, as usual, with a prayer-meeting at 7 A.M.; and at this early hour one young man decided for Christ. In the afternoon there was a meeting for men only, which will never be forgotten. Every seat was filled. Professional and commercial men, as well as mechanics and toilers of all sorts, made up the audience. In a plain, outspoken address from the words: 'Whatsoever a man soweth, that shall he also reap,' Mr. Cook spoke to the intelligence and hearts of his hearers. Several men went into the enquiry-room, and many came later and testified to good received. The last night—June 12—came all too soon. Every seat was occupied, and many persons could not get in. Mr. Cook first addressed the converts, and then made a last appeal to the undecided. The response will never be forgotten. There was a general move towards the enquiry-room —dozens and dozens passed in, until the room was over-crowded. The power of the Holy Ghost rested upon the whole audience, and God was 'mighty to save.' During the mission three hundred and thirty persons professed conversion. Men and women holding prominent positions in the town have publicly testified to the fact of their salvation. All the churches in the district have received substantial increase to their membership, and the good done has spread far and wide. People from Adelaide, Burra, Narridy, Laura, Crystal Brook, and throughout the district have been converted during the mission. Many ministers came from distant Circuits, and have gone back greatly blessed to do work for Christ.

"A large company assembled on the railway platform on Wednesday afternoon to see Mr. and Mrs. Cook start, *en route* for Broken Hill. After much tender leave-taking, the hymn, 'God be with you till we meet again,' was sung with great feeling. 'May God bless and honour His servants still more abundantly!' is the prayer that rises from hundreds of thankful hearts in Port Pirie. On Wednesday evening the converts were entertained at a plain tea, and addressed by ministers of the town, after which they were placed under their respective pastors. About one hundred and thirty joined other churches, and the Wesleyan church will receive two hundred new members. When the converts—who filled the whole body of the Institute Hall—rose and sang the doxology, the glory of the Lord rested upon us. The good work still goes on. Every day brings some new case. In three of our country churches there were conversions last Sunday, and 'still there's more to follow.' Now unto Him who loveth us . . . to Him be glory and dominion, for ever and ever. Amen!"

Writing ten days later, Mr. James says: " Every day brings to light some fresh case of good received during the mission. Many conversions have taken place among those who did not enter the enquiry-rooms. . . . .

" Our present difficulty is to find room for our people. We have more members now than we can seat in the church, and the Institute is not available. . . . Personally I am humbled before God, that unto me, who am less than the least of all saints, is this grace given. My Pentecost has come indeed. Blessed be God! . . ."

The next letter tells of the work spreading to all the country places, and of conversions in the ordinary services : " We had four conversions last Sabbath at Port Pirie," and then proceeds as follows :—

" We are so crowded out that we have decided to extend our borders. Last night we accepted tenders for the enlargement of the church. It will involve an outlay of two hundred pounds sterling and will provide accommodation for one hundred and forty additional worshippers. The work is to be begun on Monday and finished in six weeks. We are losing people, because we have no room. The people are willing in the day of power. One hundred and fifty-seven pounds have been promised already toward the two hundred pounds. The converts are turning up well. There are very few unaccounted for. The total list now reaches three hundred and seventy."

Six weeks later, the Rev. James Haslam, of Kent Town, preached sermons to crowded congregations in connection with the opening of the enlarged building. A local secular paper, sent to us, stated that the additions had greatly improved the appearance of the church, which now would seat four hundred and twenty persons, and that the congregation was to be congratulated on having raised the entire cost, two hundred pounds, during the time that the work had been in progress.

Among the converts at Port Pirie was the town-inspector or surveyor. He was led to attend the mission because of his connection with the choir. On the second Sabbath he had resolved to stay at home, but, at the entreaty of his wife, he was induced to attend the men's meeting, and was so powerfully convicted of sin that he cried out in agony of soul. Before the service closed he realised the assurance of Divine forgiveness. The following morning he called his family together for worship, and, for the first time during twenty-three years of married life, he read God's word with them, and offered prayer. His voice choked with emotion, but God was with him. That evening his wife joined the ranks of those who were on the Lord's side. The testimony of this man produced a marked effect upon the minds of others. Some came to see what power it was that had got hold of such a man; and they themselves remained to pray.

A little boy who had given his heart to God on the Sunday afternoon, brought his eight-year-old sister on the Monday evening. As Mrs. Goode, one of the workers, was entering the enquiry-room, she turned to see who was pulling her dress, and found it was Arthur. When she asked what he wanted, he replied, " I have brought Maudie, and I want you to convert her." " But I cannot convert her, Arthur," answered Mrs. Goode. " No, I know you cannot," he responded; " but you can talk to her as you did to me, and that will help her." She did talk to Maudie (what else could she do?), and both children were undoubtedly blessed. A few nights later, their mother was among the seekers; and on the Friday after the mission closed, their father found peace through believing. He was town-clerk and well known. On the following Sabbath he publicly testified, at the Congregational church, to the blessing he had received, and thanked God for the mission.

Another man attended the services on the first Sabbath, and went away apparently unmoved, fully determined that he would not attend again. Each night some member of his family urged him to go, but he as persistently refused. He had a most irritable temper, he said, and was sure he could not control it. The last night of the mission came. His wife started off to the meeting, and omitted to ask him to accompany her. This preyed on his mind.

Why had she not asked him? He would go and surprise her. He changed his clothes hurriedly, and got to the hall, to find it packed and many unable to get in. He struggled to the door, where he could hear. I was giving an illustration of an inexperienced driver being run away with by two fiery horses, until a pair of strong arms from behind seized the reins and speedily brought the horses under control. He saw in the illustration his temper running away with him, until God came to take possession of his heart and to bring it into subjection. He determined there and then to hand the reins over to Him who is " mighty to save." The struggle through the crowd into the enquiry-room was a severe test; but he reached it, and went home rejoicing, to join his wife in praising God for His great salvation.

Space fails to tell of all the interesting cases, but they include a Jew and his wife; a Roman Catholic; a father and mother, who were awakened from indifference through the loss of their two children by drowning; careless ones, who came to the mission "just to see what was going on"; aged persons, who had grown grey without being found in the way of righteousness; young men, occupying good and responsible commercial positions; and some full of sympathy and good works, but lacking the one thing needful. As an instance of good done which was not tabulated, Mr. James sends a letter he had received from a schoolmaster, who resided some miles away from Port Pirie. He and his wife had attended but one service. They did not go into the enquiry-room, but yielded at home to the spirit of conviction that rested upon them, and together sought and found

Christ. The next day the husband wrote as follows: " I am sure you will be pleased to know that both my wife and myself have decided, from henceforth, to be on the Lord's side. Personally, I have been trying to live a Christian life for the last four years, but had not sufficient moral courage to avow myself. I have found myself gradually slipping back more and more and feel that I cannot continue in this way any longer. The meeting last night showed me that I was not what I thought myself to be, and after reaching home I determined really for Christ. . . ."

But what are the permanent results of work such as this? It is said many who are zealous for a season, turn back and become worse than before. So it was in the time of Christ. " Many went back and walked no more with Him." But this does not prove that Christ had no real disciples. It was so, likewise, in the days of the apostles. John says : " They went out from us, but they were not of us; for if they had been of us, they would, no doubt, have continued with us." A revival of religion is well described in the Parable of the Sower. There are four kinds of hearers, represented by the seed which fell by the wayside, among thorns, in stony places, and on good ground. Because some seed fell on stony places, does it prove that none fell on good ground? All who profess to be converted in revivals do not apostatise. There are precious fruits that abide. A year after our mission in Port Pirie, I wrote and asked for information concerning those who had professed decision for Christ during our visit, and received a reply which will be heartily welcomed by all who sympathise with revivals.

Mr. James wrote as follows:—

"In Port Pirie the work has gone steadily on. We have had large increases in every part of the Circuit. This Circuit has now the largest membership of any Circuit under one minister in South Australia (our members are over four hundred). *Spiritually*, our churches are all alive, and many of our members are seeking and claiming a life of entire consecration. *Financially*, there is a similar progress. . . . I hope to leave the Circuit that I found involved financially, and dull spiritually, in a perfectly sound condition, well organised and doing solid work for God. To God alone be all the praise! Now, under God, this blessed condition of things is largely due to the impetus given to us by your mission. . . .

"On Wednesday, June 12th (the anniversary of the close of the mission), Mr. Claridge gave a Society tea, and invited all the church members. During the meeting held afterwards, I asked those who had been converted during your mission, or through influences resulting therefrom, to stand and sing—

> 'O happy day that fixed my choice,
> On thee my Saviour and my God.'

It set all the joy-bells ringing when quite half the people present rose and sang the hymn. *There are very few backsliders, not more than ten out of the whole number who joined our church.* We have lost a number by removals, but they have taken the fire elsewhere."

In a postscript, he says: "I forgot to mention that one of the converts has got 'safely home.' John Dowle, aged sixteen, was converted during the mission.

He afterwards went to Way College, in Adelaide, and, whilst at home for Christmas vacation, contracted typhoid fever and died after a few days' illness; but he left a good testimony behind. This death led to the restoration of his father, who had been a backslider, and now both father and mother attend our services regularly, and witness a good confession."

To Rev. T. A. James, the indefatigable pastor, the mission owed more than a little. How much his ceaseless activity and efficient organisation contributed towards its success, only the Great Day will reveal. Without his co-operation and hearty sympathy, much that we have to report would have been impossible. I take this opportunity of placing on record our appreciation of his spirit and help. The special baptism of the Spirit which he received during the mission, helped to qualify him for carrying on the work after we left. It requires the same power to keep a soul in the love of Christ, that it does to bring him to Christ. The work of the ministry is the "perfecting of the saints"; and the power that affects this, though not so conspicuous in the eyes of men as soul-saving work, may be quite as excellent in the sight of God. "Neither is he that planteth anything, nor he that watereth, but God that giveth the increase."

We reached Broken Hill on Friday, June 15th, at 8 A.M., after travelling all night. The Rev. R. M. Hunter met us at the station and took us to his home, where we remained until the mission was over. Broken Hill has a remarkable history. There have been many instances on record, during the nineteenth century, of towns and cities in all parts of the world having an almost phenomenal growth, but it is much to be doubted whether any case has ever occurred to equal that of the town and district we are now describing. About ten years ago Broken Hill was known as an outlandish stretch of the most barren and uninteresting country it is possible to imagine, such as could scarcely provide food for a single flock of sheep. To-day it is one of the most flourishing and busy centres of industry in the whole of Australasia, whose silver mines provide one third of the world's output. Some idea of the size and importance of the principal mine, called the Proprietary Mine, may be obtained from published figures. In seven years the mine produced fifty million ounces of Standard silver, and two hundred thousand tons of lead. In dividends, bonuses, etc., during that time, the shareholders received no less than six millions sterling. The average profit is now a million per annum. The normal weekly yield of silver has reached three hundred thousand ounces. During the week of our visit the yield was valued at one hundred thousand pounds sterling. The mine employs three thousand men; and, so far as human prescience can vouch for it, untold millions still lie hidden within its depths. Mining experts have the idea that, as depth is attained, the ore will become richer. Other mines exist which have not had the same success; but most are sufficiently wealthy to pay working expenses and substantial dividends. The town was incorporated in 1888, and has gradually improved, until now it assumes an almost imposing appearance. Row upon row of stylish plate-glass shop windows; huge hotels and drinking saloons, let at fabulous rents; a spacious town-hall, with its mayor in regalia; streets all kerbed and paved, and lit throughout with the electric light; a magnificent hospital, fitted with all modern improvements; a regular and copious water supply; and last, but not least, ample provision for church and chapel goers. Add to this the handsome buildings that have been erected; public park and play-ground; direct railway communication with Adelaide; and a population of twenty thousand souls: then you will be able to form some idea of the progress the place has made, and of the promise the town gives of becoming, at no distant date, the second city in New South Wales. Though situated within the borders of that colony, Broken Hill is seven hundred miles from Sydney, and only about three hundred and fifty miles from Adelaide; so that practically and geographically, and for all purposes of commerce, it may be considered as part of South Australia, especially as a large percentage of its population hail from there, and the railway they have constructed puts the Broken Hill people in direct communication with their capital.

Our church in Broken Hill is a fine handsome building, octagonal in shape, and having accommodation for eight hundred worshippers.

Both financially and spiritually we found the cause depressed. With less than a hundred members; and these burdened and discouraged because of heavy debts,—the accumulation of several years,—and with religious indifference all around, such as we had never met with before in the colonies, it was no easy task to inspire enthusiasm and expectation during the first few days. But prayer and faith prevailed; and soon there were indications of a rising tide of spiritual influence in increased congregations and many conversions.

Before the first week ended, victory was assured; and the last few days witnessed scenes of gospel triumph worthy alike of our Master and His cause. During nine days two hundred and sixty persons professed decision for Christ; the love of many who had grown cold was rekindled; scores received a baptism of the Spirit; and not least important was the encouragement the mission brought to ministers and people. One of the first to seek salvation was a noted footballer, who had considerable influence over the young men of the district. The Sunday-school superintendent rejoiced over five youths from the select class, for whose conversion he had long prayed. A mother who had recently lost her child, and had rebelled against the Divine will, came humbly confessing her sin. After finding peace and joy through believing, a man in the enquiry-room sent for his wife and daughter, who had remained in the church when he came forward. The daughter responded and sought the Lord as he had done. The next night the wife was among the seekers. A Christian man belonging to Kooringa, who had three sons converted during our mission there, was much concerned for a son who was living in Broken Hill; so he decided to come and help us, with the hope of influencing his son to attend the services. But God answered his prayer before he arrived. The lad found salvation the night his father was journeying. So runs the record in our diary of toil and triumph. A few weeks later Mr. Hunter sent some additional particulars, with a note, stating that he had verified the "cases" by actual and personal investigation. A man and his wife, with three young men boarding with them, all found Christ during the mission and joined the church. To see their smiling faces was a means of grace. Another man and wife had been Presbyterians, but rarely, if ever, attended church. He came to the Saturday night meeting for "workers," thinking it meant " a working-men's meeting." The instructions I gave to those who were to help in the enquiry-rooms impressed him greatly, so that on the Sabbath he decided for Christ. His wife followed a few nights later, being led by her husband. "There can be no doubt about the change in them both," says Mr. Hunter, "they are now anxious to bring their five children up in the fear and love of God." Another man who had been very profane in his speech, though otherwise a decent man, and a leader among the Good Templars, was converted, with his wife. They had previously gone to no place of worship. "Now," said the wife, "ours is like another home; and we are so happy." They are both meeting in class, and promise to be very useful church members. These are only specimens, but they are sufficient for our purpose. They illustrate, better than any words of mine can describe, how "mightily grew the Word of God and prevailed." What the ultimate issue will be is not for us to determine; but if one soul from Broken Hill shall ascribe to our instrumentality his or her conversion, in the day of the Lord, it will be compensation enough for the effort we made to visit that district.

With our host, the late Rev. Robert Morris Hunter,

we had much sweet fellowship. He was a man of deeply devout spirit, ever keeping the great end in view, and seeking to help others. Though far from being well, he attended all the services of the mission, and was usually among the last to leave the church. We learned to love him as though he had been an old friend, and could not help but admire the qualities of character he possessed. We engaged to maintain a life-long friendship; but shortly after we left, the illness developed to such an extent that he was obliged to leave the Circuit and seek rest. For weeks he lingered in weakness, manifesting perfect submission and trust, then he stepped peacefully into "that light of the morning when the sun riseth, even a morning without clouds." In comparing notes we found his experience particularly rich and helpful. His vivid realisation of the indwelling Christ, as a fount of light and life, and his remarkable access to God in prayer, were a great inspiration. Often we saw the face of God together, and obtained assurance of coming blessing.

Of Mr. Hunter's end a few words will be sufficient. Referring to the possibility of a fatal termination of his illness, he said: "I have no misgivings or anxiety about the issue. I should be glad to recover, to get to my work again; there is so much to be done. But I do not know what is to be, and I must just leave it all with God." Another time, when he was suffering severely, he remarked: "A little more of this and I shall be on the other side. I do not know whether I shall live or die; but I know that I am safe in the keeping of my Saviour. He saves me, and will save me. Whatever happens, I cannot choose whether to live or die. I leave it all to God, and it must be well—life or death, equally well. Praise the Lord!" In this spirit he joined "the great majority." "Still loftier than the world suspects, living and dying."

Next on our programme was a farewell service at Adelaide before leaving the colony. By travelling all night we arrived in time for the service. Old Pirie Street Church was packed to the doors; and a more enthusiastic service could hardly be conceived. Numerous letters and telegrams were sent from the places where we had held missions. Each place sent a text of Scripture appropriate to the occasion, or a suitable motto.

Representing Kent Town, the Rev. James Haslam said: "Through the blood of Jesus Christ, one until the day dawn." The Rev. W. Langsford, superintendent of Moonta, was present, and gave a thrilling account of the progress of the work there. From Kadina, the Rev. Isaiah Perry wired: "Accept farewell greetings; mission here glorious success; work continues."

The Kooringa telegram acknowledged gratefully, blessing received, and ended: "The Lord bless thee and keep thee; the Lord make His face shine upon thee, and be gracious unto thee; The Lord lift up His countenance upon thee, and give thee peace."

From Port Pirie the Scripture was Philippians i. 9–11, with the following: "Hundreds thank God for the visit, and send affectionate farewell."

Broken Hill sent a letter signed by both ministers, with kind messages similar to the others. Much was said at the service about the far-reaching influence of the work, and the impulse to evangelism which had resulted. The following resolution was unanimously adopted. It summarises and expresses the feeling of the meeting much better than any words of mine could :—

"This meeting devoutly expresses gratitude to Almighty God for the gracious outpouring of the Holy Spirit in connection with the recent mission conducted by the Rev. Thomas Cook in the Pirie Street, Kent Town, Moonta, Kadina, Kooringa, Port Pirie, and Broken Hill Circuits; in which missions more than two thousand persons have professed conversion, and a large number of believers have received the Holy Ghost. Nor has the work of conversion ended with the mission. In each Circuit the song of salvation continues to be sung by a constantly-increasing company of the saved. To Mr. Cook the meeting desires to tender its warmest thanks; to acknowledge its great admiration of, and to bless God for, his singleness of purpose and his untiring zeal in labour incessant. His coming has been to our own and other churches a timely lesson, and a sowing from which is expected an abiding harvest of good. To Mrs. Cook, his devoted wife, and true helpmeet in this sacred work, the meeting respectfully and gratefully proffers its thanks, and prays that both may have the continued protection of Almighty God in their journeyings hence, and that the harvest of their reaping may, under God, be yet more abundant and blessed."

We closed the meeting with a shout of praise, a song which we are sure the angels took up, and which reverberated in the heavenly mansions. It was the sound of those rejoicing over lost ones found. Was it any wonder that we sung the doxology over and over again? May we not well exclaim, "What hath God wrought? To Him be all the praise!"

The railway station was crowded by those who had been blessed at our meetings when we left for Melbourne on Friday, June 29th, and amid farewells of the most affectionate character, and the familiar strains of "God be with you till we meet again," we started for our new field of labour. The parting was a wrenching asunder of ties, which, though only lately formed, had grown to be both strong and tender.

WESLEY CHURCH, MELBOURNE.

CHAPTER V

VICTORIA

Melbourne—Address on Soul-saving Preaching

LEAVING Adelaide on Friday afternoon, we reached Melbourne at nine o'clock on Saturday morning. The distance is five hundred miles, which will give an idea of the rate of travelling by the best trains in the colonies. We were met at the station by the President of the Victorian Conference and other ministers, whose reception of us was as warm as the summers of their sunny land.

Victoria, of which Melbourne is the capital, was separated from New South Wales in 1851. Fifteen years previous to that there were not more than one hundred and eighty persons to people the district, which, during our visit, was occupied by over a million. The extent of Melbourne is comprised within a radius of ten miles from the General Post-Office, while its inhabitants number nearly half a million. "Marvellous Melbourne" she had been designated; and, judging from her rapid growth, magnificent broad streets, handsome buildings and superb shops, equal to any in London, we do not wonder that she should be so described. Referring to the days of her prosperity, Froude said: " Melbourne is twice as large as Adelaide and many times more than twice as rich. The population of it is three hundred thousand, who are as well off as any equal number of people in the whole world. They have boundless wealth, and as boundless ambition and self-confidence." But when we were in Australia, a change had come over the scene, as the following statistics, published by a local paper—the *Argus*—will show. "In 1891 the population of the city and suburbs was 490,896. At December 31st, 1894, it had decreased to 438,955. This shows a decrease of 51,941 in three and three-quarter years; but the exodus was much greater than that number: as the excess of births over deaths amounted to 31,170 during that period, it follows that the total loss of population to the city and suburbs had been 83,111. A year ago it was estimated that there were about sixteen thousand empty houses. Last year, 1894, the decrease was only six thousand, and the exodus may be arrested."

A colony whose exports are produced from the soil, must be in a serious condition with half its population huddled into one city. This, to a large extent, was the condition of Victoria. In Melbourne itself we found the people manfully facing the situation, and doing their utmost to retrieve their lost position; but poverty and suffering were everywhere, and the very opposite feeling prevailed to that which Froude describes. All were humbled and depressed, and much more ready to listen to our message than they would have been in the days of their prosperity. Their losses and difficulties had created a hunger for something more substantial and satisfying than the things of this world.

POST-OFFICE, MELBOURNE.

Our first mission was held in Wesley Church, which is being worked on Forward Movement lines by the Rev A. R. Edgar. By the "Forward Movement" I mean a return to the spirit of early Methodism, in adapting our measures to the needs of the times. We talk about the weapons our father used, admirably adapted to the times in which they lived; but now some of them are as much out of date as the old blunderbuss is in the army. Methodism was an adaptation of Christian energy to the needs of the eighteenth century. It was and is an evolution, not a revolution; and the Forward Movement is the same. It recognises the Divine law of adaptation, and adapts its weapons to the difficulties of to-day. John Wesley is often quoted by those who cling to rusty usages, but "those who quote Wesley as an authority against all change, are as inconsistent as the Pharisees who built the tombs of the prophets and forgot the lessons of their lives." John Wesley would never have allowed the sentimental attachment to old methods of a "select few" to interfere with necessary alterations. If congregations had declined, he would have adapted his methods so as to retain them, and not have allowed the cause to dwindle to feed the selfishness of those who would arrange the services to suit their own convenience, instead of considering the needs of the "majority outside." "The Church was founded," says Mr. Hughes, "not to protect sickly, hot-house Christians from a breath of fresh air, but to evangelise the human race. It is an army to conquer the world and the devil, not an ambulance corps to carry about lazy Christians who ought to walk on their own feet." If souls are not saved by the methods we adopt, then we must alter our methods. That is the "Church for the times," which decides to "prove all things," and to "hold fast that which is good."

This is what Mr. Edgar is doing in Melbourne. He does not adopt new methods because they are new; nor does he reject them for a similar reason. He copies those of our English missions that answer, and is flexible enough to reject those of which he does not approve. And it is wonderful how God has blessed the innovations that have been introduced. In a church, which a few years ago was practically empty, he has an average attendance now of a thousand men each Sunday afternoon; and no Sabbath passes without some conversions. The Sisterhood, rescue-work, prison-brigade relief department, and musical attractions have all contributed towards success; but the pleasant Sunday afternoon service is undoubtedly the key to the success of the mission, and is its distinctive feature.

Under the blessing of God, the chief factors in the success of the movement are:—1. The strong individuality of the superintendent, as shown in the manly, robust, and liberal way in which social questions are dealt with. 2. The fact that the subjects are always up-to-date—matters that are, at the time, engaging public attention. 3. Splendid popular music, the best that can be obtained. 4. The hearty interest taken in the work by the men themselves, who talk about the meetings and excite the interest of those with whom they work. From the report, just to hand, we learn that during the past year one hundred and eighty-seven persons knelt at the penitent form

in the ordinary services, and professed to find peace through believing in Christ. The workers are constantly meeting with people who have decided for Christ while the services have been going on. Others, awakened, have gone home and surrendered. Many letters are in their possession from people in the country, telling of renewed consecration to God while attending the services of the mission.

The report of our visit to this Melbourne mission shall be as brief as possible. With no regular congregation or families connected with the place, and the absence of young people, we had difficulties of an unusual character to contend with. But these were overcome by adapting ourselves to the situation; and, from the beginning, our work was pre-eminently blessed. After the first few days the whole Methodist population became interested; and soon the building was far too small to accommodate those who wished to hear. The special feature of the mission was the wonderful midday meetings for business men. Each day I gave an address on some aspect of sanctification. These addresses were so blessed of God that, before the mission ended, the church was filled, gallery and every available space, with Christians anxious to press into Beulah land—all hearts aglow with the manifested presence and power of the Holy Spirit. Fifteen hundred persons present at a noonday meeting for the promotion of holiness is surely an extraordinary gathering, and speaks for itself of the hunger which existed for spiritual blessing. Most of those who attended gave their dinner hour to the service, and were content to eat a sandwich as they returned to their work. Many letters are to hand from those who were blessed at the meetings. The two or three extracts which follow speak for themselves:—" I know you will be glad that it is well with my soul. I never knew what it was to have the abiding Presence with me as I have done since I attended your meetings. At one of them I gave myself fully to God; and since then my peace has been as a river. My pipe was my great stumbling-block; but since that day I have never once had the least desire for it, and previously I was a perfect slave to tobacco. Never was I more determined to live near to God and to be 'out and out' in His service." Twelve others send a joint-letter: " We, of the third Saturday meeting, want to tell you that the Lord used you to lead us into definite blessing, and that your helpful messages are still ringing in our hearts and lives."

A minister writes: " Praise the Lord! the work grows. All the suburbs are catching the fire. I received a great blessing at your meetings, and have had souls saved every Sunday since you came. I do not expect a Sunday to pass now without some deciding."

Another minister says: " I feel it a pleasure to bear testimony to the blessing I have myself received. As a result of your mission, an old quarrel has been made up in connection with our church, and now the brethren dwell together in unity. I meet many who tell me they have been richly blessed, and have felt a supernatural power creep over them when at the meetings. Many have been helped who have made no public acknowledgment. I am continually meeting with such instances."

The evening meetings increased proportionately in

COLLINS STREET, MELBOURNE.

attendance and blessing. The following are the numbers of seekers the first week :—Sunday, 33 ; Monday, 22; Tuesday, 22 ; Wednesday, 40; Thursday, 37 ; Friday, 29. But the second Sunday was the memorable day. Gipsy Smith, who was passing through the colonies on his way to America, came to our help. To relieve me he took the morning service, and the overflow meeting at night. A local paper thus describes the services of that day :—

"Gipsy Smith took the morning service to relieve Mr. Cook. The building was quite full, an event which has not happened for many a long year at a morning service. He chose as his subject the incident in Christ's life when He cast out the dumb spirit, the disciples enquiring as to why they could not cast him out, and the reply, 'This kind can come forth by nothing but by prayer and fasting.' The whole sermon bristled with tersely-put truth, straight home-thrusts and earnest appeals, varied in a most natural and easy manner by irresistible flashes of humour and the tenderest pathos. The description of the punishment of his two boys for playing truant, the callousness of the elder, and the contrition, repentance, and forgiveness of the younger, how he reassured himself again and again of the fact of his forgiveness, and then abandoned himself to the enjoyment of the restored favour of his father, brought tears to almost every listener. After the sermon, Mr. Smith sang: 'Throw out the life line.' He has a beautiful voice, which, moderated and controlled by the heart feeling behind it, finds a response in the hearts of those who listen, which words would fail to elicit. About two hundred stood for consecration at the close of this service. The afternoon meeting was for men only; and a magnificent sight it was, towards three o'clock, to see the great building packed more than full with men, many standing for want of a possible chance to sit down. What a distinctive appearance a crowd of men like that with bared heads had. The great sea of faces, whose numbers grew on you, altogether unlike any effect that could be produced by a mixed audience; and two thousand deep voices rolling out the tunes, stirred one's heart as nothing else could. As in the other meetings, they couldn't wait until the commencement, but started up singing on their own account. Gipsy Smith sang: 'The Saviour is my All in all'; and then 'Onward, Christian Soldiers' from that audience was something to remember. The Rev. Thomas Cook gave the address, a straight-out piece of personal dealing from end to end. 'Be not deceived, God is not mocked: for whatsoever a man soweth, that shall he also reap.' It is impossible to report Mr. Cook's addresses within reasonable bounds as to space. They are so full of condensed thought, trite sayings, and weighty logical arguments, and this was no exception. At the conclusion, Mr. Smith sang: 'Can a boy forget his mother's prayers?'; and eighteen sought and found the Saviour.

"Concurrently with this service, the Conference Hall was crowded with women only. Mrs. Edgar led the meeting, and spoke to mothers, urging them to give themselves to Christ for the sake of their children. Two of the Sisters sang a duet, with organ and violin accompaniment; Mrs. Mullen and Miss Palmer sang twice; and each of the three Sisters gave a short address. Three persons were saved in this meeting.

Then followed the workers' tea, attended by seventy persons, and afterwards the evening service.

"The church was filled to overflowing in every available spot long before the time of the meeting; so the Conference Hall was again opened, and soon also crowded out; no more could be packed in either. Rev. J. W. Tuckfield opened the Conference Hall meeting, while Gipsy Smith sang in the church. As soon as this was over he took charge of the meeting, and sang the same piece again: 'Come, the dear Master is calling.' 'God has given every one of you,' he said, 'a square chance for heaven. He called you by a thousand loving entreaties, by bereavement, by special invitations, such as these meetings, and now He calls you by the lips of a poor gipsy boy, who, although he never went to school, has crossed the Jordan and given himself to Christ.' At the close of this service, sixteen found the Saviour. Then as to the great meeting in the church, words fail to describe all that happened there. Mr. Cook preached from the last chapter of Revelation: 'The Spirit and the Bride say, Come,' etc. The Spirit was there in Person, His presence was manifested; and they did come at His invitation, and the preacher's, until seventy-two names had been recorded in the enquiry-rooms, and the glad hearts of every child of God danced for joy again; but there was a greater joy than theirs." Hallelujah.

At least six thousand five hundred persons attended the services that second Sabbath, and no less than one hundred and eight professed to find the Saviour—a fact which made the people "sing praises" over and over again when the announcement was made. "Probably there never was such a day at Wesley Church," said one of the workers, "certainly there never was a grander." Monday night's service was another wonderful time, church and Conference Hall both crowded out again ; and such a number of seekers that all vestries were filled to overflowing. That night one hundred and four professed to find salvation. One poor fellow, whose weakness was love of drink, rushed into the enquiry-room, crying, " If you can save me from it, I will give you all I have got. I have eighty-five pounds in the bank, but I owe a man two pounds ; the other eighty-three pounds I will gladly give to be saved from this habit." He went home "looking to Jesus." But space fails to give particular cases, though many were of unusual interest. Altogether about five hundred professed to give themselves to God, of whom not more than twenty were under sixteen years of age. We never had such a proportion of adult converts in a mission before, and certainly such a reaping time had never been known in the history of Melbourne Methodism. The air was full of indescribable spiritual electricity as we sang for the closing hymn of the mission—

"Glory, sing it again,
Glory in the highest."

It would be impossible to give more than a mere outline—a sort of bird's-eye glance—of the scenes of gospel triumph we witnessed in connection with the other Victorian missions. To describe the variety of incident and experience belonging to any one mission, would more than fill the space at disposal for the whole colony. Our readers must be content with a short account of each place we visited.

We held our next mission at South Melbourne, on the other side of the river from Wesley Church. Though three miles distant, the influence had spread, and so prepared our way that we found all quite ready for harvest. The first Sabbath showers of blessing fell; and each day the tide of grace rose higher and higher until, before we finished, over three hundred persons had pressed into the kingdom. Of these there were quite a number of husbands and wives who, either together or on separate nights, sought Christ. One of the most striking cases was that of a man of position and intelligence, who had not been in a church more than once for twenty-five years, but who boldly confessed Christ. Several others had tried to persuade themselves into various shades and degrees of scepticism; but these intellectual doubts invariably vanished when the heart was made right. One enquiry-room scene has left an ineffaceable memory. A man who had been the subject of many prayers, after wrestling for some time, at last jumped up with radiant face and shouted, "I've got it! I've got it! Praise the Lord!"

The following letter, from a local medical man, reveals how deeply and widely the influences of the meetings were felt:—

"I am the leader of the Baptist Christian Endeavour Society—the largest in the district. As a society we had been praying for your mission; and it is about our last night's prayer-meeting I wish to tell you. The previous Friday, one of our members told us that his father had been to one of your meetings and was much impressed, and he asked us to pray for him, which we did most earnestly. Last night he told us, with quivering lip and heartfelt tears of joy, that his father had found peace in Jesus, and not only so, but that his mother and sister had also been converted. We all rejoiced with him, and praised God together. Then another young man told us that in his place of business seven young fellows had received Christ, one of them being a ringleader in evil-doing; and his conversion had caused quite a sensation among the others. Another told us that several for whom he had been praying had been brought in, and of one especially, who seemed most hardened, to his great astonishment was the first to enter the enquiry-room. There were two young men present who were strangers, and they told us that they also had come out for Christ last week. To God be all the glory! I know you seek it not for yourself, but to lay at the Master's feet; and I pass these items on to strengthen your hands and rejoice your heart. . . ."

It is hard to gauge the good accomplished, because such work baffles arithmetic. Spiritual influences cannot be represented in figures; but such indications give reasonable proof of sincerity, and of the beginning, at least, of a spiritual work with enormous possibilities.

While in Melbourne, I was invited to meet the ministers of the various Methodist churches, and deliver an address on "How to preach, so as to save souls."

Upwards of a hundred were present from the city and suburbs, and a most interesting conversation followed. As I was asked to repeat the address in several other towns, I will mention some of the points I emphasised. Ward Beecher delivered hundreds of sermons before he conceived the real design of preaching. For a long period, preaching with him was an end, until he was baptized with the Holy Ghost, when he saw it was only a means to an end. Then it appeared a definite, practical thing. Preaching is only a method of enforcing truths, not for the sake of the truths themselves, but for the result to be sought in man. A sermon is good that has power over the heart; but it is good for nothing, no matter how good, if it has no moral power over men.

Our business is twofold: to turn men to righteousness, and the perfecting of the saints.

Results will vary with different constitutions and temperaments. The number of those won for Christ will be greater or less; but if men are called of God, some will be won, and others helped and blessed. Certainly, if, after years of opportunity in the ministry, nothing but barrenness marks our course, there is something wrong. Men sent of God will go about their work in such a spirit that some will bow before their force. Such men command sinners to repent, and some obey. But to succeed in soul-saving there must be *definiteness of aim.* Singleness of eye is the preacher's first and foremost need. If a man has a reputation to sustain he will accomplish but little. It is to be feared that thousands of souls have been sacrificed to sustain pulpit dignity. The people must go away saying, not "What a preacher!" but "What a Saviour!" Even ministers have to choose what they will live for. An administrator, a popular man, a winner of souls,—which shall it be? At Madeley, the very worldlings said of Fletcher: "There goes the soul-saver." If we decide to live for this, everything must bend that way. In composing sermons we must fix our eye upon what we mean to hit, and sacrifice everything that would interfere with the accomplishment of our purpose. Wesley's sermons do not compare in sublimity and style with those of Hall and Chalmers; but Wesley hits the definite mark every time, and does not waste an ounce of powder in fireworks. We must consider what is most appropriate to the need of the people, not what will please them most and win us most credit. Study their constitution rather than their palate. Reading literary essays will not avail much. Literary tastes may be gratified; but our chief business is to meet the needs of the souls. Not that I disparage the cultivation of the intellect. Christianity invites and consecrates every gift and art of which we are capable; but the human element often becomes a peril and a snare. Technical phrases are not understood. We must preach as we talk in ordinary newspaper English. Educated people are not deceived by learned verbiage. They regard inflated talk as an evidence of ignorance rather than culture. The lofty rhetorical style, so popular thirty years ago, has had its day. Plain, straightforward, simple language lays hold of the multitude. "Too colloquial," was one of the objections to my trial sermon; but Jesus Christ and common sense were on my side, and subsequent events have justified the method. "Great sermons lead the people to praise the preacher. Good preaching leads the people to praise the Saviour."

There is no eloquence like that gushing and persuasive oratory, which naturally flows from an educated man whose soul is on fire with love for souls. Of a certain D.D.'s sermons it was said : " They never could convert a sinner, because they were never meant to do it." As a rule, we secure the results we live and preach for. Nor are souls won by elaborate arguments. General Grant was indifferent to long and laboured editorials of opposition papers; but he said he hated to be stung by keen paragraphs. The fatiguing moralities, gravities, and ponderosities of the regulation sermon seldom disturb the sinner. It is the hissing bullet of the sharpshooter that brings him to his knees. "Californian" Taylor has hit upon the right principle in his chapter on surprises. The people must be surprised into thought; hence points are more effective than arguments, and illustrations than rhetorical appeals. The head, the heart, and the fancy must all be appealed to; but it is with the conscience the preacher must specially deal. Some preach about sinners instead of preaching to them. They studiously avoid being personal in the sense of making the impression on any person present that he is the man. Nothing could be more fatal to success. To our unconverted hearers, only those sermons are worth anything which single out each person, saying : " Thou art the man "; and then press upon him, and narrow his way, and hem him in, and smite him down, " until, quivering and trembling, he crouches between the Law that condemns, and the Cross that saves." Rather than :

> "Smooth down the stubborn text to ears polite,
> And snugly keep damnation out of sight,"

we must cultivate directness of appeal. Do not think I am talking about somebody else. I mean you, and you, and you. Probably such preaching will offend some; but better offend them than harden them in sin; and nothing is so hardening as the gospel if it is not responded to.

But would this style of preaching answer in regular Circuit work? No other sort of preaching does answer. Even in respect to popularity, this straightforward dealing is the best policy. To maintain our hold upon the confidence, respect, and affection of the people, we must be faithful. They despise a man in their hearts who will go into the pulpit and preach smooth things. Manly outspokenness, if united with tact, does not offend people anything like as much as is supposed. If a man is careful how he says it, he will find his congregations like best what they don't like. The harder you hit most men, the more they respect you. But they must be sure of three things: that the preacher loves them and is sincerely seeking their good; that he understands what he is talking about; and that he lives what he preaches. When such men fill the pulpits, the people will fill the pews. It is not around creeds that the people rally, but around men—men in whom they believe, and whose ministry helps them to live nobler lives.

When Dr. Joseph Cook was last in England, he was asked the difference between present-day preaching and the preaching of fifty years ago. His reply was to the effect that preaching to-day is more intellectual, but the preaching of the past appealed more to the conscience and the will. Sermons, then, consisted of introduction, argument, and application; but now the rage for short sermons leaves no time for the application, and it has had to be abandoned.

What Wesley thought about preaching without application two extracts from his journal will show:—

"My spirit was stirred within me at the sermons I heard (at Glasgow) both morning and afternoon. They contained much truth, but were no more likely to save one soul than an Italian opera."

"This very day I heard many excellent truths at the kirk (Aberdeen); but as there was no application it was likely to do as much good as the singing of a lark."

The kind of preaching a worldling likes is that which will permit him to keep on living in sin, and still feel fairly comfortable. The preaching I recommend will save such men, or drive them away from our sanctuaries. This was the effect of the Master's ministry; some were saved, and others "walked no more with Him."

Desperate earnestness is also absolutely essential. None but those who have a settled, unconquerable purpose will succeed in leading men to Christ. A feeble resolution will soon be overcome. Is there one, whom difficulties dishearten, who bends to the storm? He will do but little. Both God and difficulties yield to the man who is thoroughly determined. Souls were never more difficult to win than now. Those who think they are going to get great victories at small cost are mistaken. Sin was never more aggressive. It has boldness, skill, and resources such as it never had before. Soul-saving means "labour" of body and brain, but we have this comfort, that the hardest work gives most happiness afterwards. Determination not to fail is all important. If sinners do not yield to first appeals, we must try again.

Appeal and re-appeal until they do come. Some expect to fail, and they do; but others, by the assurance and confidence they possess, create faith wherever they go. Let us never be discouraged. God seldom uses men who have lost heart. We must preach as dying men to dying men. Of Murray M'Cheyne a Scotchwoman said: "He preaches as if he is a-dyin' a'most to have you converted." The *British Weekly* attributes the lack of pulpit effectiveness to a decay of passion. Undoubtedly, intense yearning for souls is one of the conditions of powerful preaching. It is only when we feel deeply that others begin to feel. We need to be at white heat to make any deep impression. Few can follow an abstruse argument, but all can *feel*. Hence it is that exhortation is quite as high a gift as preaching. "The preacher calmly inculcates truth upon the intellect, the exhorter sways the sensibilities which lie nearer to the will. It is greater to *move* than to *teach*. A candle can illumine an ironstone rock, but only a furnace can melt it. Gospel preaching cannot be counterfeited. An unregenerate intellect, well read in theology and trained in rhetoric, can preach a popular sermon, but exhortation cannot be imitated. The soul must be aglow with the live coal from off the Divine altar. No sham is possible here. The pathos of a soul on fire from above, speaking through tears and sobs, prayers and entreaties, is an irresistible power which the Church cannot afford to lose. This gift is not from the schools. Culture cannot bestow it. It must be sought for in the upper chamber, alone with God." Peter did not preach, but testified and exhorted, on the day of Pentecost. Few among us can exhort as the old preachers did; and yet by this gift the refined and the vulgar can be reached more than by any other. Many have told me that, when they were on the exhorters' Plan, they led more souls to Christ than they have done since they entered the ministry.

What to preach. Preach the Word. We waste time when we defend the Bible. If we preach it, it will defend itself. All successful preachers deal largely in the true sayings of God. Wesley's sermons are simply solid Scripture utterances. Of Chalmers it has been said that his sermons " held the Bible in solution." A peculiar energy always attends the Divine Word. It is "quick and powerful, and sharper than any two-edged sword." Let us not be afraid to preach sound doctrine. A revival that is not founded upon the truths of the Bible is like a blaze of pine shavings, and will end in smoke. There was this difference between the preaching of Wesley and Whitefield : while the latter proclaimed, with amazing unction, the plainest and simplest truths regarding sin and the Saviour, reiterating those in every place all his long career; Wesley, on the other hand, dealt extensively and perseveringly in full doctrinal state-ments, opened up and pressed home upon the conscience. Whether the converts of our missions remain steadfast or not depends much upon the type of ministry under which they have previously sat. Where there is decay of moral conviction concerning law and penalty, there is always corresponding weakness all round. Maudlin sentiment, and laxity in reference to future punishment, have produced much of our modern indifference to the claims of religion and authority. If we hesitate to declare the danger, the people will hesitate before they believe in it. It may not be popular to teach that God will punish sin, but the Book says He will, and we must declare it. There is creeping in among the churches a sort of rose-water theology that would exclude all the sterner truths. John Bunyan warns us to beware of Mr. Clipscriptures; and the warning was never more needed than it is to-day. On these subjects we must have convictions, or our preaching will become careful and timid, without moral earnestness and without power. Our hearers intuitively perceive whether or not we believe what we preach. "What the world wants is a faith; and for the man who can unhesitatingly say, 'I believe,' and can express his belief in simple, homely language, there is, and will always be, both a platform and an audience."

Souls are not saved by "ifs" and "hows" and "buts" and "whys"; we must speak as the Master did, "with authority." Dogmatic preaching is always powerful, because half our hearers believe what their ministers believe, and because they believe it. If we keep to what the Book teaches, we shall not go astray. The sterner truths should occupy the same proportion in our utterances as they did in the Master's deliverances. It may be necessary to use different phraseology. There is no advantage in becoming victims of a mere traditional verbiage; but the great truths held and taught by our fathers concerning sin and penalty, we must teach, emphatically as they did, or we shall lose our hold of the people. What we think of the Atonement depends greatly upon what we think of that which made the Atonement necessary. The man who has felt his guilt most deeply, and realised most keenly his exposure to the pangs of the "second death," always appreciates most the value of Christ's infinite sacrifice. Unless the Law is preached, men will not see their need of a Saviour, nor will they value as they should do, Christ's great work. " Preach the Law for conviction," says quaint John Berridge; " use its carving knife. Moses will lend you a grindstone to sharpen it on. When sinners cry out for mercy, bring out your Christ. He will be acceptable then." Take away the honest, hearty belief that without Christ souls are irretrievably and eternally lost, and you have broken the mainspring of evangelistic activity. Practical indifference always follows loss of vitality in evangelical faith.

Then as to our method of work. Success or failure depends much more upon these than most preachers seem to realise. " He who has the greatest variety of baits, will catch the most fish, and of most kinds." If a man goes angling, he takes with him, not the bait that would be most pleasing to his own palate, but the bait the fish like best. Why do we not, in religious work, apply the same principle of common sense? If one plan does not answer, we must try another, and keep on doing this until we succeed. It is well to meet prevailing notions of decorum as far as is consistent with the work being done; but mere sentimental attachments to old methods should not be allowed to interfere with necessary improvements. Methods and principles should not be confounded. In principle we cannot be too fixed, but in mode we should be pliant. Wise men are wedded to usefulness, not to method. Unless we cultivate fertility of expedient, the Church will continue to crawl along slowly, while all the world is moving at electric pace.

Above all, we must have the Pentecostal power. With this, the weakest among us will accomplish more for God than the strongest will without it.

My views on this subject will be given in a subsequent chapter; but what I urged particularly was, that the baptism is a sort of initiatory rite to a life of Pentecostal service. Before we receive our Pentecost there is not much service worth the name. With the promised baptism the apostles entered upon a new phase of life and work. And so it is to-day. Christian life begins at Calvary, but effective service begins with the baptism of fire.

These points, variously illustrated, comprised my address, and were exemplified in the missions I conducted. They are the secret maxims and principles of my life and work; and the longer I live the more am I confirmed in the opinion that God has given me these views in regard to the best method of winning souls. Nor was this message to the ministers in vain. Several who heard, and were helped and blessed, carried the flame to districts we were not able to visit. One wrote to say the hints (in detail) relating to method had supplied the missing link in his ministry. He had had several conversions each time he had tried the plans I suggested, in his after-meetings, and was filled with a new joy and hope.

Before leaving the colony of Victoria, we held missions at Geelong, Ballarat, and Bendigo; and then proceeded to Tasmania.

"To every man his work."—MARK xiii. 34.

"One earnest soul fired with the love of Christ may set a whole Church on fire. Nearly all the greatest revivals have commenced with individuals. The Acts of the Apostles is chiefly a record of individual labour of men fired with the love of Christ. Philip finds his man; Paul finds his man or woman, and then the work spreads to Samaria, etc. Christ's best work was personal. If we would seek for a fresh baptism of the power from on high, and then carry our live coal of love to the dead and the dying, what a stir we should make in our churches. All would be workers then; and Scripture and history fully establish that this is the Divine method of saving the world."

"Heaven's gate is closed to him who comes alone;
Save thou a soul, and it shall save thine own."—WHITTIER.

CHAPTER VI

VICTORIA AND TASMANIA

Geelong—Ballarat—Bendigo—Hobart—Launceston

GEELONG occupies a commanding position on one of the prettiest parts of the Western coast-line, about forty-five miles from Melbourne. It is a quiet, thriving town in the midst of an extensive agricultural district, with a population of twenty-five thousand. One-sixth of the people are adherents of our Church, for whose spiritual needs we have five ministers stationed in the town, and as many churches. Our visit was anticipated with large desires and expectations. The mission commenced on Sunday morning, July 29th, when, to a crowded church, I lifted up God's standard of holiness. It was a delightful service; the Spirit seemed to shed down upon us the atmosphere of heaven. Goodwill and sympathy were everywhere. Not a discordant note was heard during the whole mission. On the Sunday evening the service was held in the Mechanics' Institute, with the result that three hundred more persons heard the message than could have done had we remained in the church. At the close of the day, it was found that more than seventy had professed conversion. This, for a beginning, was most encouraging; and blessing increased as the mission progressed. A quiet, deep feeling pervaded the town. Each night the hall was filled with attentive hearers. The hardest hearts and the most tender were touched alike by the Spirit of God. Men who had grown old in sin, and children knelt together among the anxious, but the majority of the seekers were young men and women from our own families. Christians came to be refreshed; some came long distances, sacrificing money and business, to seek the better treasure Jesus gives. At our last afternoon holiness-meeting, at least a thousand persons gathered who were seeking for full salvation. Many went away to prove that there is a rest *here* where the soul can enjoy, without interruption, the fulness of Christ's love. Not a few fires were lighted in that service, which were borne away to distant places to kindle revivals, of which we have been glad to hear since. The direct result of the mission was that three hundred and seventy-five persons entered the enquiry-rooms and professed to find the Saviour. The indirect result will probably never be known. The vibration of that one battery may have for its circuit a continent or a world. Among the best fruits was the encouragement given to the workers at a mission-room in one of the worst parts of the town. For years the work had continued, and, in some respects, successfully. Crowded congregations were secured; the people improved socially, but few comparatively had been converted. This was cause for much anxiety and prayer. When our mission was announced, the workers felt that this ought to be the reaping time after so many years of patient sowing. Accordingly, a circular was drawn up, conveying a personal invitation to attend our meetings, and delivered to all who attended the mission-room. A portion of the Mechanics' Hall was reserved for them, and many came. The result was just what was desired. Forty of the regular attendants at the mission-room were saved, and the workers' hearts filled with joy. After twelve months, particulars were sent as follows:— "Eleven of the converts had slipped away, but six had returned again, leaving thirty-five out of forty genuine cases, all meeting regularly in class." But forty-five others had decided for Christ during the year, including ten habitual drunkards, and several Roman Catholics. Some of them had not been in a place of worship for years. Whole families had turned to God, until the entire aspect of the neighbourhood was changed. Writing of this work, the superintendent minister says: "There is a complete revolution in the district where these people live. Some of the conversions are remarkable for their clearness. Between fifty and sixty have undoubtedly been truly converted. The change is complete. 'Old things are passed away.' All is new. And the work is going on splendidly."

At the first Sunday morning service a lady of respectable position, who had been for some time a seatholder in our church, was deeply moved, and at the holiness-meeting, on the Tuesday afternoon, entered into light and liberty. Her conversion was singularly bright and definite. She went home and told her husband of her new-found joy, with the result that he also became decided. She accompanied him to the enquiry-room to confess Christ, and to tell of His goodness to her. Her testimony to her friends of the great change in her heart and life brought two others to seek the same blessedness. This is one of the many cases where conversion was the direct result of teaching concerning the higher Christian experiences. Nothing was then said about conversion; the possibilities of faith proved the attraction. An odd story has been sent me of one man who was saved,—a wild desperate fellow,—a Greek by birth. His wife asked for a ticket for him for the men's service. He promised he would go; but, when Sunday arrived, he changed his mind, and said he would go to the Salvation Army service instead. In the course of the morning he drank fourteen half-pints of beer to nerve himself for the service. After dinner he was brushed up and went out. He returned home about five o'clock, and told his wife he had been at our service. "You haven't," she said. "But I have," he rejoined; "and what's more, I've been down into the cellar." (By the cellar he meant the room under the stage, which was used as an enquiry-room.) "Surely you haven't," said his wife. "Oh, yes, I have," he said; "and here's my ticket"; and, diving down into the pocket of his coat, he produced the card containing instructions to seekers which we give to all who enter our enquiry-rooms. "All that glitters is not gold," I know; but we have known many real and abiding triumphs among characters such as this.

Another man was the son of a Primitive Methodist minister. He greatly ridiculed the mission when he heard it had been arranged for. On the Sabbath he attended and went away angry. Next day he had to go into the country to work for the whole week, and said he was glad to get away out of reach of the services. As God ordered it, the people for whom he had arranged to work were not ready, so he was obliged to return home again. Though he did not like the services, he came that night, and all the week, until the love of Christ conquered him, and he could resist no more. None sought the Lord more earnestly than he did, nor did any seem to find peace more clearly. He has joined the Church as a member; and attributes the work of grace in his heart to the halo of prayer, which since his birth has always surrounded him. Notes of other interesting cases lie before me, but I must refrain from quoting them.

The labours of the Christian Endeavour Society helped much to secure the results we report. The Society consists of young people who have each signed the following pledge:—

" Trusting in the Lord Jesus for strength, I promise Him that I will strive to do whatsoever He would have me do; that I will pray to Him and read my Bible every day; and that, just so far as I know how, throughout my whole life, I will endeavour to lead a Christian life. As an active member, I promise to be true to all my duties; to be present at, and to take some part in, every meeting, unless hindered by some reason which I can conscientiously give to my Lord and Master, Jesus Christ. If obliged to be absent from the Monthly Consecration Meeting, I will, if possible, notify to the secretary my reason for absence."

It would be difficult to exaggerate the importance of this movement, adapted as it is to fill the gap between the School and the Church. It has ramifications all over Australia, and is the great hope of those who are interested in the young people. In thousands of instances it has proved itself to be a sort of halfway house to the Church; and, as a training school for young workers, the movement is simply invaluable. We found its members full of life and energy; and at most of the places we visited they were among our best and most reliable helpers. The Society has tapped sources of real power, which are found in the ardour and enthusiasm of youth, as no other movement has ever done. We were glad our Church had taken up the idea, and was pushing it with heartiness and success.

That the class-meeting has suffered by the introduction of the Endeavour Society none will deny. Many young people cannot give two nights in the week to religious services, and most prefer the Endeavour meeting, with its freshness and variety, to the class-meeting, especially if the latter is formal and stereotyped, as some are. The difficulty has been met, in some churches, by the appointment of the president of the Endeavour Society as a class leader, and attendance at the Endeavour meeting being regarded as equivalent to attendance at class. Other ministers, who were unwilling to recognise this compromise, have had to deal with the awkward problem of having scores of their best and most earnest young people outside Church membership, because they are not attached to some Society class. Happily, the Conference is alive to the importance of the question, and is disposed to adapt its measures to the difficulties which have to be faced.

When the Endeavour movement was first introduced into Australia, fears were expressed lest the sense of obligation to our own Church should be loosened by the frequent intercourse with other churches which it encourages. Such fears, however, have proved to be groundless. The organisers of the Society have done their utmost to encourage denominational loyalty, and we can bear testimony to the attachment of Methodist "Endeavourers" to their own Church. They have been taught that they can do the best work by concentration of energy, such as finds its most convenient expression among their own people. The narrowness of denominationalism has, in itself, elements of usefulness and opportunities of service, such as would be impossible except in connection with our own Church. At the same time, occasional contact with Christians of other persuasions is very valuable, and must be an increasing factor in religious life. It enlarges our view of genuine religion, gives us wider sympathy and mental breadth, and opens our eyes to the fact that the number on the Lord's side is far greater and more powerful than we ever supposed. Whilst our own Church is best for us, and attachment to it healthy and good, we do well to remember that we do not by any means possess a monopoly of spiritual life and power. There are many choice Christians who are not of our persuasion doing noble work for God, contact with whom would be an inspiration and a source of strength.

Associate members of the Endeavour are those who, while they are not willing to avow themselves decided Christians, are willing to put themselves under Christian influences. Habitual attendance upon the meetings is required of these, but not participation in the meetings. Their connection with the Endeavour keeps them from going astray in the interval between leaving the Sunday school and joining the Church. It was from among this class we gathered some of the best results of the Geelong mission, and towards which the active members contributed so extensively. The Geelong Christian Endeavour Society is one of the strongest and best organised in Australia. This is due largely to the indefatigable members of the Hitchcock family, to whose many excellences there is to be added the crowning glory of eminent Christian character. To Mr. and Mrs. G. M. Hitchcock we owe a debt of gratitude which we shall never be able to repay for the hospitality they provided, and their overflowing kindness. After the mission they took us to their sea-side residence at Barwon Heads for a few days' rest, which did much to invigorate us before starting at Ballarat.

Ballarat is an active, flourishing city, with a population of about forty thousand. It is situated in the midst of a rich gold mining district, and, "in point of architectural excellence and general civilised city comforts, it is certainly the metropolis of the Australian goldfields." Since the first gold was discovered, in the year 1851, Ballarat mines have yielded the precious metal to the value of sixty millions sterling. The noise of the quartz mills, which greets the ear day and night, indicates how all the business interests still throb with vitality. The Botanical Gardens impressed us profoundly. Of these Froude writes: "Such variety, such splendour of colour, such sweetness, such grace in the distribution of treasure collected there, I have never found combined before, and never shall again." But the Carrara marble statuary has left on our minds the deepest impression. One piece purchased in Rome, the work of Professor Benzoni, said to be worth £4000, was worth a day's journey to see. It comprises three figures, representing father, mother and infant, escaping from Pompeii. Four bas-reliefs illustrate the eruption of Mount Vesuvius and the destruction of the city, and seem to mark the very moment when "the earth and surging seas gave signal" of the warning. This, and the other beautiful works of art, all of the highest class, and thoroughly educational, were gifts to the town by generous donors.

No fewer than forty places of worship exist to provide for the religious needs of the community. We found the same craving for special revival services there as elsewhere; but, owing to a mission held by Gipsy Smith a few weeks before, in which five hundred professed conversion, we had not the same success as at other places. It is never well for one evangelist to follow quickly on the heels of another. Each has his own method of doing things; and even when the first has got a good hold of the people, the services are almost sure to run down under the second, however suitable and successful he may previously have proved himself to be. Those ready for the Kingdom had been gathered in, and we were left with the hardened cases. The results, however, were better than we had dared to expect. We were permitted to witness a great quickening of religious thought and feeling, and nearly two hundred persons sought salvation. The interest in the meetings was general and hearty, and many were awakened to the solemn issues of life as never before. Several of the conversions were the result of appeals from relatives and friends in other towns, who had themselves been the subjects of the Spirit's operations in our former missions. A woman who had been converted at South Melbourne urged her friends, by letter, to seek the peace and joy she had found in Jesus, and to attend the mission with that object. Her testimony and appeal led to the conversion of an aged mother, three married sisters, and her own daughter, who was visiting Ballarat at the time. How cheering it is that every soul won for the Saviour becomes at once a source of additional power to His cause—a new centre from which good shall radiate to the surrounding masses. Whole families were saved, and persons of all ages and conditions. The foundations of men's hopes were tried as by fire. Some in the Church saw that they had been building "on the sand," and found hope in Christ. Not a few who had been Christians for years, thanked God for a brighter sky and a stronger faith. One of the afternoon meetings was pre-eminently a season of blessing. After an address on the fulness of the Spirit, I asked the congregation to repeat the words: "The fulness of the Spirit for me now." "*Purchased* for me," "*Offered* to me," "*Accepted* for me," "*Now*." Many, with their souls as well as with their tongue, said, "*Now*." It was no flash of enthusiasm, but a God-inspired faith. Under a gush of irresistible feeling we claimed "the fulness" *there* and *then*. After an interval of some weeks, one wrote to tell of the abiding character of the blessedness that service had inaugurated, in language that reminded one of Samuel Coley. Speaking of the time when he claimed the fulness under a sermon preached by Thomas Collins, he says: "That 'now' stirs me yet. Nor ever since that memorable time has my faith dared to procrastinate or say anything but 'Now' to all the sanctifying offers of the promise-keeping God."

Only definite preaching produces definite results. Unless we set before the people distinct points of attainment, there will be no marked and decided progress. Indefinite exhortations to men to lead sober, righteous, and godly lives, produce no satisfactory result; but the preaching of the necessity of immediate regeneration leads to conversion, present and real. So it has been found among Christians; if we show them plain, definite steps, they attain definite experiences. Among the Moravians, where full assurance of faith is much insisted on, there are more instances of high religious faith than in almost any other denomination. When a definite point is presented to the believer as immediately attainable, prayer is no longer at random. His heart goes out toward the blessing he is seeking and there is no rambling of petition. All the energies of the soul are aroused and concentrated, and definite blessing soon follows. In preaching, I try to make a point, and allow things to crystallise around it. This leads to definite and specific results, such as conversion and entire sanctification.

During our first week in Ballarat, we stayed at the house of the Hon. David Ham, one of the local Upper House representatives—a self-made man of indomitable energy, and as fine a character as we met with in the colonies. The Rev. Samuel Knight provided hospitably for us the second week—a man of marked individuality, richly evangelical as a preacher, and a loving, tender, and devoted friend. We left both homes with regret, abundantly thankful to have been introduced to the friendship of these brethren, and their devoted wives.

Bendigo is not so large a place as Ballarat, and is

REV. SAMUEL KNIGHT.   HON. DAVID HAM.

situated more in the interior of the colony. Mining is the chief occupation of the people; and, in Australia, such communities are the most difficult to impress with spiritual truth. Our work, at first, was no light task; labour, hard and unyielding, was demanded, but the promise was found sure, and blessing came. The spiritual rain was as abundant as the natural rain, which interfered much with our congregations. The young people were first to seek the Saviour; but, as the power increased, all classes came to share in the hopes and enjoyments religion offers. Men who had been seeking—not always with the best success—the corruptible treasure, found contentment in the satisfying portions God so freely bestows. The aged came with the remnant of their wasted life. Prodigal sons, feeding on husks, bethought them of the plenty in the Father's house, and arose and came to Him, to find welcome and peace.

Christians confessed unfaithfulness, and had restored to them the joy of God's salvation. Ten days went by all too quickly, leaving behind them, as the fruit of our visit, rejoicing converts, a quickened Church, happy homes, and an increased respect for God's work and His workers. The resident minister sends particulars of one case of almost picturesque interest. "It is that of a Roman Catholic who, one evening, was standing on the footpath in front of the church, talking to some one, when he heard the singing, which he describes as the sweetest he ever heard in his life. He determined to go in, but as he ascended the steps the singing ceased, and just as he took his seat you commenced to speak, and he became at once so interested that he felt riveted to the spot. He says he learned more concerning the way of salvation during that one hour than in all the forty years of his life before; and while he sat there he was led out of a great darkness into a marvellous light; and although he did not go into the enquiry-room, he there and then went direct to Christ for salvation. He now clearly realises Christ as his personal Saviour, and has fully withdrawn from the Roman Catholic Church. In joining our Church he expresses the hope that he may be able to proclaim far and wide the wonderful change which has come into his life." We complain, sometimes, of the number who leave us and go to other churches; and certainly we lose more than we gain, but we do gain some. Nor are those who join us from other churches to be despised. Some of the best Methodists I know, came from the Church of England. The converse is also true, some of the best in the Church of England went from us. There is no brighter crown on the head of our Church than that which represents the influences she has set forth to quicken and bless other churches.

In addition to the one hundred and ninety-four persons who entered the enquiry-rooms at Bendigo, there were many who were blessed in their pews, as the following letter from a working-man will illustrate:—" I have much pleasure in informing you that I am one of the number, who, through your instrumentality, received Christ at Bendigo. The first Sunday evening of your mission I was sheltering from the rain in one of the church porches, quite unconcerned about my future spiritual welfare, when, by accident, I heard you speak of Christ, and urge sinners to flee to Him for refuge. I did not enter the church that night, but decided to hear you again on the following night. While doing so, I thank God, He spoke peace to my soul. The light from heaven shone then, and it shines now, upon me. My reason for writing is that you may know of my conversion, which you might never hear of except in this way. I did not go into the enquiry-room, because Christ came into my heart as I sat in my seat. Since my conversion I have made known the change, and am now endeavouring to persuade my companions to follow my example. Farewell! God bless you, and watch over you in your travels." To be used of God in work like this is the greatest privilege of my life. Most heartily can I subscribe to those words by Thomas Collins: "Soul-saving is next to heaven. Indeed it gets more of my thought than heaven does." If men did but know the joy it gives to turn sinners to righteousness, all would be willing to take the lowest place among those who have part in this work, which is the only one that angels envy. Samuel Rutherford used to say to his flock: "My witness is above, that your heaven would be two heavens to me, and the salvation of you all as two salvations to me." It is more of this spirit the churches need.

We left Melbourne for Tasmania on Friday, September 7th, 1894, and shall not soon forget the hearty grasping of hands and the tender good wishes and expressions of friendship of those who had come to the wharf to see us embark. Our steamer bore us quickly over the beautiful bay to the sea, where we met with what is called the "Rip," and old Neptune gave us a rough reception. After a sleepless night we found ourselves at the entrance of the Tamar. We had a delightful trip up the river to Launceston. There, we took our seats in the train for Hobart, which was reached in the evening. On the platform, in spite of pouring rain, quite a little crowd was gathered to give us a warm welcome.

Tasmania is called "the garden island." Certainly it is a lovely spot,—nearly the size of Ireland,—comprising mountain, lake, and river, reminding one of many parts of Scotland, while its climate is unrivalled for salubrity. Here, Methodism has found a home for about three quarters of a century, and now claims sixteen thousand members and adherents. Hobart has a population of about twenty-seven thousand. It is situated on the river Derwent, amid surroundings eminently picturesque. The river is wide enough to be called an estuary, with shores bold and wooded, and delightful sandy beaches, and a background of hills or mountains in immediate proximity. The majestic aspect of Mount Wellington, which rises abruptly to a height of four thousand feet, almost from the city, cannot fail to impress the most apathetic observer. Hobart was laid out in the old convict days, when Tasmania was better known as Van Diemen's Land. Most of the roads were made by the prisoners, who also erected the principal buildings. This accounts for their substantial character, and the English appearance of the town. Relics of the convict days were everywhere, and many were the sad stories told us of the cruelties to which the prisoners were subjected. At Port Arthur the prison buildings were still to be seen just as they were abandoned in 1877. Our first church in Hobart was built by convict labour.

Methodism was introduced by Sergeant Waddy and by a few other godly soldiers of the 58th Regiment. The governor of the colony placed at the disposal of the trustees bricklayers and labourers, and found all the timber and lime. Opening sermons were preached by the Rev. Benjamin Carvosso in the year 1826. The present church, which will seat

HOBART FROM THE BAY.

twelve hundred worshippers, is a fac-simile of Wesley's Chapel in City Road, London. Sir John Franklin laid the foundation stone in 1837. We have now in Tasmania more than one hundred churches, and thirty ordained ministers. This, among a population not exceeding one hundred and fifty thousand, indicates progress which is surely cause for thanksgiving.

We found the Christians at Hobart hearty and united. Not only were our own people full of expectation, but those of other denominations. All worked together, and all shared in the blessing, More than two hundred professed conversion during our visit, but the encouragement given to workers, and the quickened spiritual life of Christians, were among the best results. The attendance increased at every meeting for the promotion of holiness, and the work of grace deepened until the spiritual influence was profound. Several ministers came from distant places, and went back from the meetings with a new power to lead souls to the Saviour.

One wrote afterwards as follows:—"It gives me great joy to tell you that in my Circuit we are having an outpouring of the Holy Spirit. I told you it was my intention to hold services. We commenced on Sunday week, and I had the joy of reaping morning, noon, and night. We had seven seekers in the morning, six in the afternoon, and two at night. From Sunday to Friday fifty-six have decided. Many men have yielded to God. One old man, seventy-four years of age, was converted on Thursday. We are now in the midst of the work. At our last service we had fifteen seekers. I am continuing all this week."

Our meeting for men only was an imposing sight. About a thousand were present, and their sturdy voices made the old church ring. No doubt heaven also sang for joy when twenty-three fine fellows sought the Lord with repentance. One kissed my hand as he left the enquiry-room, and said with deep emotion, "God knows I have been bad enough. I hope this will be the beginning of a new life." Referring to the converts' meeting, held after the mission, one of the stewards wrote: "We need have no fear of the future of our Church when we can witness such sights as this." Scores were there to testify of their joy and gladness from hearts brimful of new-found salvation in Jesus. The resident minister wrote: "A new vigour has been given to the people generally."

One of the young ministers who attended the mission from a distant part of the island, told us that he had been lending a copy of my *Early Ministry*, written by Rev. H. T. Smart, among the people of his church, with a view to creating interest in our visit. In one home, where the mother was an earnest Christian, a younger son had but recently decided for Christ. His elder brother made it as difficult as he could for the lad to be true to the Saviour. The book was lent to that home, and the mother read it aloud each evening to the assembled family. The elder son's interest was so awakened that he could not wait for the usual evening's reading, but would have the book for himself. Reading it led to his conversion; and he was one of those who attended the Hobart mission, with several others who had been interested and blessed by the same means. The writer of one of the letters from Hobart bears a similar testimony: " I feel I must write to express my thanks for the great blessing I received at your afternoon meetings. I have been a professing Christian for some years, having joined the Congregational Church at my home in Yorkshire, and cannot remember the time when I did not love God, but if I had known the meaning of those beautiful words, 'The blood of Jesus Christ, His Son, cleanseth us from all sin,' how much happier my life would have been, and how much more useful. I did not receive the blessing until your meetings were over, though I was very anxious; but having bought a copy of your *Early Ministry*, I found the Tuesday afternoon's address there, and while reading it, the light came. Now, thank God, I am rejoicing in a full salvation. How strange it seems that one from so near the dear old home should come out here to lead me into the light. Will you pray that I may be used for the Master."

The Church has yet to learn the value of the printing-press. So great is its power that it is already hard to say whether the pulpit or the press wields the greater influence. There can be no question that the press commands the greater audience; and Satan's agents are not slow to take advantage of it. How is it we are not more alive to appreciate its possibilities in extending the Master's kingdom?

Our treatment at Hobart was especially cordial and generous. Friends seemed to vie with each other which could be kindest. During our week of rest we were taken to see some of the lovely scenery for which the district is noted. We saw much that we shall never forget; but the view from Mount Wellington was most remarkable. No pen can do justice to the scene. The grand panorama of river, estuary, and ocean, and mountain succeeding mountain, which is disclosed as you ascend, is beyond description. It was a veritable wonderland, and amply recompensed for the trouble and discomfort we had sustained in climbing the height.

Some of the trees on the side of the mountain were of such circumference that eight of us taking hold of hands could barely reach round them. The few days which we took for recreation to visit the scenes of beauty with which the Creator has so richly endowed that neighbourhood, did much to revive our energies for the Launceston mission, which commenced the following Sabbath.

Launceston is distant from Hobart about one hundred and thirty miles. It is the second largest town in the colony, and has a population of seventeen thousand. Situated beautifully on the river Tamar, it is eminently English in its appearance, architecture, and surroundings. The people, too, are quiet and refined, such as are met with in our English cathedral towns. We held our mission in Patterson Street Church, a fine, Gothic structure, capable of accommodating quite a thousand persons. Elaborate preparations had been made in the shape of a covered way from the church to the schoolroom, which was used for enquirers, and a platform for the choir. The choir consisted of singers from all the evangelical churches, to the extent of a hundred voices. Ministers and people were of one heart; and all classes were ready to do their utmost to promote the success of the undertaking. From the beginning large congregations assembled; and the tide of religious feeling rose, until the whole city felt its influence. Not a few were converted who had been seatholders for years, and had passed through many revivals; but among the young people the best work was done. The number of these who came out boldly to confess Christ is one of the brightest memories of that mission. Sixty-three entered the enquiry-room at the first young people's service, some of whom belonged to our leading Methodist families. We heard of at least one home from which young folks were converted, who afterwards brought their parents to the Saviour. "It made our hearts jump for joy," writes another, "to hear the straight, manly way in which several of the young fellows spoke at the converts' service." Ten days soon passed by, leaving behind them more than two hundred who had professed conversion, and a general elevation of the spiritual life of God's people. At times the awe, and the irresistibleness of impression, were such that almost all the unconverted persons present were swept into the Kingdom. Care was taken to guard against the danger of aiming at immediate rather than permanent results. In all our missions, depth and reality were the first and chiefest consideration. Repentance and the sterner doctrines were faithfully preached, and workers instructed to aim at thoroughness in dealing with enquirers. Teasing, decoying, and all other doubtful measures were studiously avoided. The work was accomplished by the use of simple and honest means, which God's Word either directly prescribes or fairly sanctions.

One of the chief benefits of our missions is to bring back churches to first principles. There is danger of neglecting the old-fashioned doctrines of ruin, redemption, and regeneration. If men are evolved from the apes, they cannot have a sinful nature, and do not need conversion, but rather education. In our missions the fact of sin is demonstrated; for, every night in the enquiry-room, there are many who feel its guilt and burden, and seek deliverance from its power. The fact of conversion is also proved; for, each evening, men and women are made new creatures in Christ Jesus. Who can doubt the fact of redemption when numbers are daily experiencing its power, and rejoicing in its blessings. " And, beholding the man that was healed standing with them, they could say nothing against it." Those who are privileged constantly to witness such effects in changed and renewed lives want no *new* gospel. Most blessedly have we proved that the gospel hath its old power yet. " Truth is mighty everywhere. The love of Jesus touches hearts everywhere. The blood cleanses everywhere. Faith triumphs everywhere." Hallelujah. We made our home, during the mission at Launceston, with the Rev. F. J. Nance, whom we had known in England. He is principal of the Ladies' College, a first-class educational institution, where the children of some of the wealthier families of our people are trained. It was under the ministry of the father of Mr. Nance that I received my first religious impressions. Many reminiscences of old scenes and faces were brought back as we talked about the old country, of those still with us, and those " lost awhile."

After the mission we spent a few days with Mrs. Reed, of Mount Pleasant, the widow of the late Henry

Reed, of Harrogate and Tunbridge Wells, well known in England as the friend of the Rev. Alexander M'Aulay, and an earnest evangelist. Mr. Reed came to Tasmania when quite a youth, and, by dint of industry and ability, soon rose to a position of prominence and wealth. Mrs. Reed has a spacious and beautiful home, where she is always glad to welcome those who are on the King's business. On the Sabbath I preached twice at one of her farms, or sheep runs as they are called in Australia. Many of the country people who attended the services evinced considerable feeling, and several professed decision for Christ.

We had now finished our work under the auspices of the Victorian Conference, and had arranged to proceed immediately to New South Wales. Writing in advance, I said: "The God who has blessed us so richly where we have already laboured will not fail us in your colony. What He has been, He is, He will be"; and so it proved.

But, before entering the territory of another Conference, let me introduce to my readers the most striking personality with whom we came in contact among the Victorian ministers. There are others to whom I should have liked to have done honour had space permitted, but John Watsford, better known as Father Watsford, possesses an indisputable pre-eminence. Throughout Australian Methodism his name is a household word; and among other Christian communities he is better known than any other Wesleyan minister. Converted to God in early life, he consecrated all the force and vivacity of his nature to the service of Christ, and was the first candidate for the ministry recommended to the English Conference from the Australian colonies. In 1844 he was sent as a missionary to Fiji, where he learnt what was meant by perils among the heathen. Belonging, as he did, to the advance-guard of the pioneer nobles who rendered such conspicuous and heroic service to the cause of Foreign Missions in Fiji, he had for his colleague John Hunt, of beloved memory, whose imperial saintliness and enthusiasm for God have seldom, if ever, been surpassed. Owing to the failure of his wife's health he was compelled, after ten years' service, to return to Australia. There he was eminently successful in winning souls, and soon made his mark as a recognised leader of all forward movements in the Church. Within a period of sixteen years he occupied the Presidential chair twice, with credit to himself and advantage to the Connexion. As General Home Mission Secretary for Victoria he rendered conspicuous service for eight years, consolidating and extending Methodism in a manner that made those years an epoch-marking period in the history of the Church.

The great themes upon which he has delighted to descant during a ministry of over fifty years, have been pardon, purity, and power. By advocacy, at conventions and missions, here, there, and everywhere, he has led thousands into these experiences. The younger ministers have caught his spirit; and probably no man in his own line of specific revival work has done more to start a "school of prophets" than John Watsford. Though now a supernumerary, he is still, "in labours more abundant," leading more souls to Christ than any other man we heard of in the colonies. Our intercourse with him was most refreshing, and as profitable as it was inspiring. He believes, as we do, that there are revivals and revivals, and that only those begotten of prayer are worth anything. The only true revival is of the Holy Ghost—"times of refreshing from the presence of the Lord." This is the supreme need. Revival within the Church first, and then the salvation of the world. When we were leaving the colony, Mr. Watsford wrote: "You will have members of all our churches in and around Sydney at your meetings; and I hope the Lord will give you such a message concerning holiness that they will carry the holy flame of love away with them and set their churches on a blaze. We do need a revival of holiness in the Methodist Church everywhere just now. Low spiritual life in the Church is felt in connection with a work like yours in this way: an evangelist comes along and the Word is with demonstration of the Spirit and with power. Many are converted and the Church is aroused. But the evangelist goes; and after a few weeks, things settle down into the old rut, and some of the converts wander away into the world, and others, greatly hindered, and never helped at all, by the frequent entertainments of various kinds now so often provided by the Church, form their ideas of religion from what they see around them, and have little or no power as witnesses for Jesus." All other soul-winners teach the same thing. Said Charles G. Finney, shortly before his death: "If I had strength of body to go through the churches again, instead of preaching to convert sinners I would preach to bring up the churches to the gospel standard of holy living."

"Let not regard for any man," said John Wesley to Mr. Merryweather, "induce you to betray the truth of God. Till you press believers to expect full salvation now, you must not look for any revival."

"Not by might, nor by power, but by My Spirit, saith the Lord of hosts."—ZECH. iv. 6.

"I once said to myself, in the foolishness of my heart: 'What sort of sermon must that have been which was preached by Peter when three thousand souls were converted at once?' What sort of sermon? Such as other sermons. There is nothing to be found in it extraordinary. The effect was not produced by eloquence, but by the mighty power of God present with the Word." How many have felt, if they have not said, what Cecil thus gives expression to!

CHAPTER VII

NEW SOUTH WALES

Bathurst—Waverley—Stanmore—Newcastle

THE Rev. Thomas Adamson acted as secretary to the Committee appointed by the Victorian Conference to make arrangements for our missions under its auspices. Writing to the *Methodist Recorder* describing the work, he concluded with the following observations:—" For some reasons it may be regarded as unfortunate that we have had so many evangelists and distinguished preachers just at the same time. Rev. John M'Neill, Thomas Cook, Gipsy Smith, and Canon Carter, with Dr. Talmage thrown in, is rather a big order, and involves somewhat conflicting thoughts respecting men and methods; but it has proved the truth of the Book, 'Every man in his own order.' They have all got that for which they have laboured— the evangelist has the garnered sheaves, the lecturer the memory of crowded audiences, and the eternal day will reveal what sort of work it is.'"

Though it did seem strange that so many of us should have arranged to visit Australia at the same time, we are decidedly of the opinion now that our missions benefited rather than otherwise by this arrangement. This was especially the case when we followed the Rev. John M'Neill. Mr. M'Neill has a marvellous power in breaking up hard ground and sowing the gospel seed, but, as is well known, he does not hold after-meetings to bring those whom he has influenced to an open confession of Christ. The consequence was, wherever our mission followed his in close proximity, we found numbers of persons quite ready to avail themselves of the opportunity of confessing Christ which our after-meeting afforded, and who were glad of the help our workers could give them in explaining more fully the way of salvation. Thus in the providence of God, Mr. M'Neill helped to prepare the way for some of the glorious ingatherings we rejoiced over. While we do not wish to criticise the methods adopted by good and able men, we still think that Mr. M'Neill's mission would have been even more successful than it was, if he had instituted some means by which anxious enquirers could have been brought in contact with ministers and other workers, who could give the necessary advice and instruction, at that critical period in their religious history.

"The after-meeting is simply an arrangement suggested by common sense and experience to prevent truth from losing its grip upon souls. The net already cast, it drags to shore; the driven nail, it clinches; the hot iron, it hammers into shape. That is the philosophy of it in a nutshell; and this sensible and rational means the Spirit abundantly uses and approves."[1] That eminent soul-winner, the Rev. Charles G. Finney, writes: "I had often felt the necessity of some measure that would bring sinners to a stand. I had found that, with the higher classes

[1] Dr. Pierson.

especially, the great obstacle was fear of being known as anxious enquirers. I found also, that something was needed to make the impression that they were expected at once to give their hearts to God; something that would call them to act as publicly as they had in their sins; something that would commit them to the service of Christ. When I had called them simply to stand in the congregation, that had a good effect, and it answered the purpose for which it was intended; but, after all, something more was necessary to bring them from among the ungodly to a renunciation of sinful ways and a public committal of themselves to God." But, in addition to the benefit arising from such open confession of Christ, the enquiry-room makes provision for needful, quiet, and intelligent instruction. All our workers are carefully chosen, and instructed concerning the best methods of dealing with anxious persons. After the workers have done their part I give a sort of general address, taking typical cases and dealing with them, answering objections, correcting errors, and leading enquirers as a body into the way of peace. The great point to be remembered in dealing with seekers is to keep their eyes fixed upon the Saviour, and not to stand in the way ourselves. In churches that are built to save souls the enquiry-room should be one of the first considerations, and easily accessible from all parts of the building. Preaching deals with men in the mass; but they are converted one by one. With rare exceptions, unless the Word preached is followed by personal dealing it does not convert. For this reason the value of the enquiry-room is now almost universally recognised.

Our first mission in New South Wales was fixed

for Bathurst. To reach that town from Launceston involved a four days' journey through some of the most magnificent scenery in the colonies. We crossed the Blue Mountains, which rise to an altitude of four thousand feet, and of which David Christie Murray says: "The landscape seems scarcely of this earth at all. Form and colour are alike unaccustomed, alien. I have travelled much in my time, but have seen nothing to which I could liken it."

Bathed in a lovely blue haze, which some atmospheric peculiarity imparts, tower majestic peaks, sometimes ranged in one continuous succession, at others so riven by the mighty hand of Nature, that precipitous walls and dizzy cliffs rise straight up hundreds of feet from the wondrous untrodden valleys beneath. Over these tear mountain-torrents, some of them broken, long before their descent is completed, into the finest prismatic-tinted sheets of spray. Gently-sloping spurs are here and there, fairy-like glen-gardens of the choicest ferns and wild flowers, while weird effects from the clouds and mountains add to the charm of the scene, and everywhere Nature is at its sublimest and grandest. What we saw created an impression which will never be effaced from our memory.

Bathurst is a small but growing town of nearly ten thousand inhabitants. It is situated on a fertile plain about one hundred and forty-five miles from Sydney, and was once a convict station. Now it is the centre of a large agricultural district, and in close proximity to goldfields which still produce considerable wealth. The town is well laid out, and is healthy and bracing. Our reception was enthusiastically kind. The mission was one of the best of the series, remarkable alike for spiritual power and far-extending interest. A local minister thus graphically describes it: "The people came! They kept coming in increasing numbers from the start to the finish. And what a finish it was! Nay, thank God! it is not the finish yet. We are only pausing to look on the battlefield and count the slain. We shall not soon forget these last ten days. Never in the history of Bathurst has there been such an overpowering of the Spirit. Pulpit and pew have shared alike in the glorious gift, and we have our hands open still for more. Last night our church was indeed packed to listen to the message. Nothing new! yet news. They talk about 'old truths in a new light.' That is what has been the case here. We have heard of 'holiness' before, and the unconverted have heard of salvation; but during the mission both converted and unconverted have heard 'news' concerning these subjects so convincing as to set their hearts bounding with joy. There has been an almost entire absence of noisy demonstration, but, in its place, has been a quiet irresistible power, conscience-awakening, life-demanding. The power in the message we have seldom so felt. At times we have forgotten the messenger. . . . We have got at the secret of his success. It is the 'power' in him. He needs no witness at our hands. May God use him more and more. Mr. Cook takes charge of the mission entirely, and the ministers have been glad it is so. The workers have devoted themselves to carefully following his instructions, with unmeasured benefit to themselves and the seekers. The aim being to excite deep and serious thought, he has only applied such tests to the congregations as were necessary, and has kept to his purpose throughout of not allowing injudicious interference with the pew. The use of the *Hymnary* by a large and deeply-in-earnest choir has been a powerful auxiliary. Many of the choir will henceforth sing for Jesus only. The meetings that appear to have been most characteristic have been the meetings for men on the Sunday afternoon, the meeting for women on the Wednesday, and those for the promotion of the higher spiritual life. To the men the arrows of the Lord were pointed and very straight. To the women the message was one of tenderness and faithfulness, and chiefly dealt with their responsibility in reference to their children. Out of sixteen women who came out for Christ at that service, were eight who had recently experienced trial and loss through bereavement. The meetings for holiness were notable for glory and for grace. May God help us to keep on 'reckoning ourselves dead unto sin.' The manifestations of the outpouring of the Holy Spirit are abundant and satisfying. There is a great deepening of spiritual life. This is not the result of morbid excitement or hysterical feeling. It is the outcome of deep conviction and settled principle. Two hundred and thirty-seven names have been taken of those who sought guidance in the enquiry-room. We have not included in these upwards of sixty children between the ages of eight and fourteen. The members of other churches have been blessed. More than fifty gave their hearts to God from the Church of England. Notably have backsliders returned to God. It has been a *good* time. We are praying that the same results may follow in every place where Mr. Cook goes."

At one of the services eight men, each above thirty years of age, professed conversion. At another, two young men who had come twenty-five miles to attend the mission were saved; and they told afterwards how, on the journey, one of their horses had been seized with illness, and rather than be disappointed they left the horses and walked the remaining ten miles. As there was not time for tea when they arrived, they came hungry to the service at which God met them. One was the son of a sainted minister and grandson of another minister. The other had been prayed for by his mother for many years. She was present at the service when he was converted, and was filled with adoring gratitude. Quite a heap of letters lie before me, received from those who were helped and blessed. A few, as specimens, must suffice. " For several days I have had the impression that I ought to write and tell you how much I owe, under God, to your visit to Bathurst. For many years I have felt the necessity of being cleansed from all indwelling sin, and have sought the experience again and again. The point at which I stumbled was, namely, the want of simple "do nothing" faith. When listening to your address on 1 John i. 7, I saw clearly, that on the condition of full surrender to Christ, and just taking him at His word, the blessing I had so long desired would be mine. I was encouraged to trust myself entirely to Him, or, as you put it, to step out on the promise, though it might appear like stepping on the seeming void. I did this and found the 'Rock' under my feet. On the afternoon of the last day of the mission I received the blessed assurance that I was wholly the Lord's. Never shall I forget the Divine manifestations of that service. Since then, I have realised a rest of soul never before experienced, and have been able to witness for Christ with freedom and confidence altogether new. I know that Jesus does save me every moment; and He who saves keeps. Praised be His name! I find it beneficial to define my position frequently during the day, and as I do so, the Holy Spirit bears blessed witness within . . . ." Another letter from the same writer tells of the inauguration of a meeting for the promotion of scriptural holiness. Twenty-five were present at the first meeting, most of whom bore witness to the all-cleansing power of the blood of Jesus. The letter concludes as follows:—"The rest of faith, simple and constant, brings a peace and joy indescribable. The Holy Spirit is unfolding the truths of Scripture to me in a most gracious manner. Since I have been brought into this Canaan of 'perfect love' it has been my greatest wonder that all Christians do not claim their privilege in Christ Jesus. . . ." Another letter says: "Mr. James met the class, of which I am a member, for tickets on Thursday last. It was a precious season, and my soul was richly blessed, as I was enabled to testify to the power of Christ to save from all sin. The words of counsel from Mr. James were as from a heart brimful of Divine love. It is not a breach of confidence to say that he dates a new era in his religious experience from the first holiness-meeting you held in Bathurst. The blessed change is noted by all. He preaches as never before. . . ."

The next letter was received six months after the mission had concluded. It tells of an increase of fifty-seven in the membership for the quarter, and of many still remaining on trial, of general prosperity throughout the Circuit, and ends with further testimony of personal blessing. " Six months have rolled by since I claimed entire cleansing by faith in the blood of Jesus, and they have been blessed months indeed. I think the experience becomes increasingly delightful. Such freedom does Christ's presence give; 'free indeed' is the word. His service has lost all its irksomeness. No longer do I need to whip and spur my laggard soul to the throne of grace. And when there, He grants me such blessed manifestations that, at times, it is almost as much as I can bear. The word of God has a new meaning; the Holy Spirit often speaks to me through portions that were previously sealed. Do help me to praise the Lord. . . ."

There are no results more cheering than the cases of those who were true Christians before, but who, at our missions, were led to surrender themselves more entirely to the Lord, and entered into a virtually new life of happy service in His vineyard. Of cases like these we have heard many times from Bathurst alone. Nor were any more blessed than the pastor himself, to whom reference has already been made, the Rev. Charles E. James. We stayed at his home, and shared his joy in the special baptism of the Holy Spirit which he received. His hearty co-operation made the mission what it was. Without him, we could not possibly have secured the universal sympathy and united and whole-hearted action which were such important factors in the work. The following letter reveals the Spirit in which he continued " to push the battle to the gate." " We had a good day on Sunday. Such a communion service had never been seen in this town. God was blessedly near the whole time. I asked the people who had not taken the sacrament before, or those who had neglected the Lord's table, who were moved in their hearts to re-dedicate themselves to the Master, to let that act be to them what coming to the enquiry-room had been to others—the sign of their decision for Christ. I feel so thankful to tell you that many did so, and now date their new life from that service. It was a time of deep feeling. Nine times the spacious rail was crowded. There was mighty power again in the evening; the church was very full. I am an unskilled fisherman and drew in the net before it was full. Two came out for God, and many more are, to my personal knowledge, almost persuaded. We are looking after the people— all the enquirers have been visited. Our people have a mind to work and are still expecting large things from our Father. Not until the Great Day will it be known what God has done for us in Bathurst through your instrumentality. . . ."

Several months later the Rev. W. G. Taylor, the newly-appointed minister, wrote : " The work holds well here. Brother James has done his utmost to conserve the fruit you gathered.' Thus some plant, others water, but God gives the increase.

To God be the glory for " stretching forth His hand to heal " (Acts iv. 30).

At the close of the mission, we took a brief trip to

the Jenolan Caves before starting in Sydney. These lie in the heart of the Blue Mountains, about a hundred miles from the metropolis. From the great variety of extraordinary shapes and brilliant colours in the stalactite and stalagmite formations, and from the numerous natural phenomena contained in their dark recesses, they are justly regarded as one of the wonders of the world.

No pen can convey any adequate idea of the dazzling splendour of these treasure-houses of nature, much less shall I be able, in the short space at my disposal. Involuntary expressions of delight constantly escaped the lips of our party, as they were introduced from one beauty to another of what seemed like fairyland. Stalactites of all sizes and colours and thickness abound, some being transparent, others resembling alabaster; while the sides of the caves are often adorned with delicate, stony drapery of every imaginable description, the splendour of which can only be appreciated by those who have seen it. The electric light, which is now in use throughout the caves, shows off their beauties to great advantage. A perfect blaze of light occasionally greeted our eyes when the myriads of crystals were illuminated. The prismatic forms were simply wonderful. Our visit to these marvels and glories of nature filled us with a sense of the majestic presence of the Infinite, and gave us enlarged ideas of the boundlessness of His resources.

We reached Sydney on Saturday, October 27th, and began work at Waverley, an important suburb, the following day. Summer was just commencing, and the heat was intense. Mosquitoes welcomed us as they do all newcomers. Lumps and blotches soon appeared where they had fastened their fangs. These irritated to desperation, and sometimes opened to a sore; but these were among the little difficulties. Our health was sustained, and God was blessing the work; so we were thankful.

Before describing the work in Sydney, some information concerning the place will be interesting. The city is named after Viscount Sydney, who was Secretary of State when the territory was taken possession of in the year 1788. It is the capital of New South Wales, and the site of the first British settlement in Australia. The first pioneers consisted of about a thousand persons, chiefly soldiers and convicts; but the population is now estimated at three hundred thousand—a remarkable record for a new country, especially as Sydney has been the parent also of so many other cities. It would be difficult to imagine a locality more obviously suited for a great metropolis. It stands on the shore of a harbour, which, whether for beauty of scenery, or adaptation as a fort, is unrivalled. As a mere picture, the harbour is one of the loveliest we have ever looked upon. In speaking of it, Anthony Trollope says: "I despair of being able to convey to any reader my own idea of the beauty of Sydney harbour. I have seen nothing equal to it in the way of land-locked scenery—nothing second to it. It is so inexpressibly lovely, that it makes a man ask himself whether it would not be worth his while to move his household to Australia, in order that he might look at it as long as he can look at anything."

It is described by Froude, in his *Oceania*, as the

WAVERLEY WESLEYAN CHURCH.

largest and grandest harbour in the world. As the eye wanders from the entrance to the city, a succession of picturesque and beautiful landscapes come under review. The irregularity of the shores, the luxuriant verdure with which the hills are clothed, the innumerable villa residences nestling cosily on the slopes of the hills, which form the general outline of the bays, surrounded by exquisitely laid-out gardens filled with plants and fruits from almost every clime, form a panorama of singular beauty. Within the harbour are a hundred or more of bays, inlets, and creeks, so as to give a charming variety. Beyond the water are jutting corners of land, then again of water, and then again of land. Several islands add to the grandeur of the scene, and merchant ships scattered here and there, and warships and huge ocean steamers, with ferry boats and quite a flotilla of sailing and rowing boats, yachts, and steam launches. These, combined, form a perfection of beauty such as we were never tired of looking at, and which has been justly described as "one of the sights of the world."

Sydney is about seven miles from the open sea. It contains many handsome buildings; but the streets abound in curves, and are irregular, rendering it much more English-looking than other Australian cities, such as Melbourne and Adelaide, which are built upon the inartistic chessboard plan.

Among the best ecclesiastical buildings is our Wesleyan Centenary Hall, built on the site of the venerable York Street Church. It was opened in the year 1888, and cost more than thirty thousand pounds sterling. Over the centre arch of the main entrance is a representation of John Wesley, and, on either side, emblematic representations of Britannia and Australia. Seating accommodation is provided for one thousand six hundred persons; but it is estimated that it will hold two thousand five hundred. The interior and galleries are decorated with considerable taste. The hall is the headquarters of the Sydney mission, which is worked on Forward Movement lines with most encouraging success.

We expected to find a goodly number of aboriginal natives in such towns as Sydney and Melbourne; but in this we were disappointed. During the whole of our visit to Australia we did not meet more than half a dozen pure aboriginals, except on one occasion in Queensland, when we went several miles to see a native "station," a sort of home provided by the Government for those who care to stay there. Some thousands do exist in various parts of the continent; but they are rapidly dying out in the presence of a superior race. They are very much lower in the scale of humanity than the natives of New Zealand, being almost nude, ignorant of the use of metals, having no houses worth the name, and rarely attempting to cultivate the ground. Like most savages they are fond of liquor; and were it not for the strict laws prohibiting the sale of intoxicating drinks to them, they would, doubtless, much sooner become exterminated through their own excesses. The sad fact impresses itself upon the traveller that little can be done to improve these people, and that they are doomed to disappear before the new and sturdier races that have conquered them. As I have before stated, even the gospel has met with very moderate success among them as an elevating agency.

Trade in Sydney was much depressed during our visit. Hundreds of men were out of work. Many of these were sleeping in the open air each night, because they had no homes to shelter them. All the labour problems which cause anxiety in England are beginning to appear in the colonies, and the same difficulties exist.

Methodism in New South Wales was regarded, until recently, as somewhat behind the other colonies in energy and enterprise; but since the inauguration of the Forward Movement in connection with the Centenary Hall it has been as "go ahead" as in any of the sister communities. If its progressiveness is more deliberate, it is because the colony has been longer settled, and they go about their work more quietly, but are none the less earnest. Our missions were held at Waverley and Stanmore, both fashionable suburbs of Sydney. At the former place we have the finest church edifice of New South Wales Methodism. Some feared lest the building might interfere with the work; but among a prepared people architecture is never any difficulty. God's people were waiting for the harvest—looking for the opening of the "windows of heaven," and on the first Sabbath, expectation was more than realised. That first day more than seventy avowed their allegiance to Christ. Of the progress of the mission another shall speak, whose testimony is the result of personal observation.

Some extracts from the report of the pastor are as follows:—" To all human appearances, scores have been converted who might not have been converted under the ordinary ministry. What joy has been in our church the last few days! The absence of noise and mere animal excitement; the deep and gracious influences of the Holy Spirit resting upon all, compelled men and women not accustomed to these things to say, 'This is a true work of God.'

"Since the mission commenced, two hundred and ninety persons have professed conversion. The holiness-meetings have been seasons of greatest blessing. The expositions of the nature of sanctification, the way of its attainment, and the hindrances to the work, have been much appreciated. The whole mission has been unique. It has been a mission to the Church, and the Church has felt it to be such. One of the most pleasing features has been the conversion of young men. These are capable, in the strength of Divine grace, of setting Waverley in a flame. In many homes, the salvation of such a band of young men has been a cause of joy and delight never before experienced. All the churches in the neighbourhood will derive benefit from the mission. To God be all the glory."

The work at Stanmore was equally satisfactory. Joy, surprise, and gratitude blended there as they did at Waverley. "From the very commencement," wrote one of the ministers, "it was apparent that God was with us; and the progress of the work has but intensified the consciousness of God's presence, and produced a deeper interest and a deeper sense of the Divine presence and power. From large to full, and from full to crowded, congregations has been the order, amply proving that the evangelist and empty seats do not keep company. It was an inspiring sight to see the large church packed in every part by those who were eager to hear the message of salvation. The old truths concerning sin and salvation, this was the story; and what a result its faithful declaration has brought about! The first day was marked by many conversions; and this has been the case at every evening service during the mission. Believers, too, have been quickened and built up and brought into closer communion with God and to a complete consecration to His service. The number of conversions can never be taken to represent the full result of such a work as this; but in respect to numbers the result has been wonderful. Altogether two hundred and fifty-seven have given in their names as having been converted. The fruit of the work is invigorated Christians, converted fathers, mothers, husbands, wives, sons, and daughters, and substantial help financially. What can we do but thank God and say, 'What hath God wrought!'; while we pray that our experience may strengthen the faith of our friends to whom Mr. Cook is going."

Not the least gratifying result at Stanmore, was the decision for Christ of twenty and more of the youths from Newington College, of which Rev. James E. Moulton, of Tongan fame, is principal. Three of Mr. Moulton's own children were among the seekers, as were, also, the sons and daughters of several other ministers.

A letter from Bathurst asked for prayer for a son, and he was one of the first to avow himself on the Lord's side. Another seeker was a divinity student, preparing for the Presbyterian ministry, but who had never realised Divine forgiveness. He found peace and joy through believing. Two day-school teachers, several prominent seatholders, and outsiders not a few, were among the trophies won for the Master. At Waverley, after a middle-aged man had found salvation, he told of the circumstances which led him to decision. His son, who was a university graduate, had been converted during our mission in Melbourne. After his conversion, he had written home telling of his new-found joy, and urging his father to attend our services. "I was astonished to get the letter," the father said; "it was so unlike him, and his request that I would write and tell him how I stood in reference to these things quite troubled me. He will be so glad to know that it is all right with me now." And he hastened home to write the letter. One incident was of melancholy interest. At the Waverley young people's service, I happened to say, "How surprised we should be if we knew who among this congregation will be called to meet God first." A young man present turned to a lady sitting next to him with the remark, "Shouldn't we!" little thinking that he himself would be the first. The lady to whom he spoke sent me particulars of his death within ten days after we had left, and these facts. Time is short and duty is large. How important it is that we should always be living up to the best that is in us. "My candle is almost burned out, and I shall not get another," was the reply of one who was asked why she worked so unceasingly for God.

> "'Tis not for man to trifle. Life is brief
>   And sin is here:
> An age is but the falling of a leaf—
>   A dropping tear.
> We have no time to sport away the hours,
> All must be earnest in a world like ours."

During our visit to Sydney I was invited by the President of the Conference to preach the official sermon to the members of the two district Synods, who were assembled for their annual meetings in the town. The service was held in the large Centenary Hall, which was well filled with ministers and laymen. My subject was: "The Pentecostal Baptism." God graciously helped me in explaining this to be the indispensable condition of success in Christian work. The mighty victories of the early Church were won in the power of the Holy Ghost. Nobody ever was, or ever will be, saved, only through the preaching of the gospel. It is the gospel applied and enforced by the Holy Spirit that saves men. The work is spiritual, and only spiritual power will accomplish it. The Pentecostal baptism will bring Pentecostal results. Power is a Person, and that Person is God the Holy Ghost. God does not hire out His attributes, as some imagine, He comes to our hearts Himself. If we want power we must seek Him, and He will work through us. The apostles had received a measure of the Spirit before Pentecost, but Pentecost made an unspeakable difference. It is one thing to have the Spirit, but quite another to be filled with the Spirit. We claim to be sharers of Pentecostal privileges, but how few possess the Pentecostal power. There must be a Pentecostal experience possible to us, similar in kind and degree to that received by the apostles and Church of the first century, because we have the same promises they had, and some whom we know are richly endowed with the priceless gift. Pentecost was simply a pledge and earnest of still further and fuller manifestations of God to man. The experience does not come to all in the same form. The Holy Spirit may come as a mighty rushing wind, or descend as the summer shower, or distil as the gentle dew, but in either form His coming fills the soul with life and light and power.

The baptism of the Spirit will inspire us to the maximum of effort possible to us, and enable us to accomplish all the work God means us to do. There is more of any man with this fulness of God than of the greatest man without it. All are fitted by the Spirit's baptism for their own life's work. Unless He is in us, the fire of love, the light of assurance, and the power of unction, we are criminally weak for whatever work God has called us to do. It makes a man willing, as well as fit, for his work. "Here am I, Lord, send me" was the result, in Isaiah's case, when he received the fiery baptism power with God and men. God-inspired courage and enthusiasm for soul-saving are other characteristic features of the experience. Much better it would be for the world if the Church would cease making weak efforts to save it, and wait upon God for this power. With this we shall accomplish more for God in one year than in a hundred years without it. If we spent half as much time in positive prayer for this power as we spend thinking about it, there would not be workers enough to help those who were seeking their way to Jesus. These are some of the points I elaborated, and which embody my teaching on "How best to help God to save His world."

Nothing was more encouraging than the manner in which the New South Wales' ministers welcomed "the stranger from afar." In acknowledging the sermon I preached, they described it as "timely and helpful," stating, also, that several ministers bore testimony to the good they had received. The following assurance of welcome was sent with a resolution of thanks. "We desire to offer to the Rev. Thomas Cook a cordial welcome to New South Wales, to assure him of our prayerful and brotherly sympathy, to praise God for the encouraging success which has attended the missions he has already conducted, and to express the fervent hope that his work in other parts of the colony may be still more abundantly blessed." It was in the same spirit which this resolution manifests, that we were received everywhere.

We held missions at Newcastle and West Maitland, after finishing at Stanmore and Waverley, with the result that five hundred additional seekers were registered.

Newcastle is seventy-five miles from Sydney, and is the centre of the coal mining industry of New South Wales. It contains a population of ten thousand, and, in maritime importance, is the town next to the capital. Our church not being large enough, willing hands transformed the Olympic Racing Hall into a mission-hall for the occasion. As the result of considerable effort, the biggest, but not most attractive, hall in Newcastle was made nearly as comfortable as a church. Many a race had been started there for a bauble, but we saw scores start there for the "crown." We can hardly say that the city was carried by storm, but the "slain of the Lord" were many, both in and far around the city. Every service was blessed with visible results. Some, "dry-eyed and calm," vowed allegiance to God, because such was reasonable and right; others shouted lustily in distress and in praise. Families rejoice together; some parents welcome *all* their children to the second fold; and in other homes husband and wife now agree. Our host told us, before we left, that fifteen of his family and connections had been converted during the mission. The last service was by far the best. Fifteen hundred, at least, were present, and all shouted for joy as the converts stood to testify what great things the Lord had done for them. The results were a surprise to many, but "the elect" know the secret. "Glory be to Him that sitteth upon the throne, and unto the Lamb, for ever!"

Here let me raise my protest against a custom very prevalent in England of sending to Australia the ne'er-do-wells of our respectable families. Nothing astonished us more than the number of these we met who belonged to families we knew. It is all very well to say, "There is room enough in Australia, send them there and give them another chance," but is it fair to Australia to send this cancerous element into the midst of their young and healthy national life. Damaged character, like dead meat, soon becomes putrid in the colonies. Where restraints are few, and facilities for going still faster to the devil abound, is hardly the place to send those who have disgraced themselves. If such cannot retrieve themselves in England there is still less probability of their doing so in Australia. I speak strongly; because, in Australia, we met several of these fast young men whose presence was an evil, the extent of which no man can divine.

We found the Church at Maitland sadly world-pressed, sluggish, and dull; but even there our covenant-keeping God made bare His wonder-working arm.

More than one hundred and eighty were helped in the enquiry-rooms, and believers received a great uplift. Perfect love is what the churches need. I preached it continually, and bore witness to its reality. Many "saw from far the beauteous light," some "inly sighed for its repose," and a few claimed their heritage. Perhaps the best result at Maitland was the conversion of a score of young men, who have since found various spheres of usefulness. Writing of them, the local pastor says: " We have quite a stock of speaking talent now, and have no lack of workers to supply appointments in the country. Most of the young men give promise of being useful Christians in the future." From the young men themselves I received the following communication, some three months after the mission: " A number of the converts of your late mission in this town having formed themselves into a Young Men's Christian Association (consisting already of over seventy members), take this opportunity of expressing their heartfelt thanks to you as the means, in God's hands, of leading them to accept Christ as their Saviour, and also to inform you that they are still holding on their way, although many have much to contend with, yet they believe that He who saved them can keep them, if they will but trust in Him. They are seeking, by Divine help, to bring others to enjoy 'like precious faith,' and share in the same blessings. They will ever remember, with fervent gratitude to God, your visit among them; and will also pray that God may make you a blessing in the future as He has done in the past." Then followed the signatures of the committee who had prepared the address. We have heard, since, that several of these young men have become local preachers. How can we doubt either God's presence, God's word, or God's power? When He is with us, there is no difficulty but may be surmounted; no enemy but may be conquered; no sinner but may be saved. The Maitland mission ended with the year 1894, and closed one of the grandest years of our lives. During that year we travelled seventeen thousand miles; I conducted three hundred and forty-six services, in connection with which five thousand five hundred persons came forward as anxious enquirers. How many of these were really converted only the Great Day will reveal, but we have reason to believe that, in the case of a great majority, the work was deep and thorough. Though thankful beyond measure for such trophies won, yet, as we faced the new year, our hearts thrilled with Xavier's dying prayer: "More, Lord, more."

CHAPTER VIII

NEW ZEALAND

Auckland—Wellington

OUR next sphere of labour was the land of the Maoris. New Zealand is situated twelve hundred miles distant from Australia. To reach Auckland, which was our first landing-place, we sailed from Sydney, on Christmas-eve, in the *Alameda*, an American vessel, bound for San Francisco, but calling at Auckland for mails. During Christmas-day and the three following days, we were "in perils on the sea" and "in weariness and painfulness" such as we are not likely soon to forget. The passage usually occupies four days; but, owing to the storm, we were twenty hours late when we reached our destination. The official report stated that the gale was the worst the vessel had experienced for seven years. We were especially grateful to God for His preserving care when we learned that only a few weeks before, while travelling the same route, a large passenger steamer had been wrecked, and more than a hundred lives lost.

New Zealand is mainly comprised of two large islands — North and South Islands — with Stewart Island in the extreme south; the area is almost equal to that of England, Scotland, and Ireland. From its extensive sea-board it resembles closely the mother country. Auckland, the largest city, has been called the "Naples" of New Zealand, because of the beauty of its situation. It stands on the east side of North Island, on a lovely stretch of water branching from the Hauraki Gulf. The approach through the gulf is most picturesque. The town rises steeply from the waterside of a land-locked bay. Behind it is Mount Eden, an extinct volcano; and within ten miles of the city the cones of nearly sixty other extinct volcanoes may be counted. Mount Eden is now covered with grass, but with a heap of slag at its base, as if it had cooled but a few years ago. Half the city stands on rock, which was once fluid lava. Most of the volcanic hills in the neighbourhood were once fortified strongholds of the Maoris. The ships at anchor and at the wharves indicate extensive commerce. Not far from Auckland are vast Kauri forests of great value. The Kauri pine takes eight hundred years to grow, and produces the best timber for all purposes which grows anywhere on the globe. The trees are valuable, also, because of a peculiar gum which they produce, and which is exported in large quantities. This gum is a deposit, not of the living trees but of the dead ones. It is usually found several feet below the surface of the earth. It looks like amber, and is used chiefly in the manufacture of varnish and ornamental articles.

Auckland is well laid out, and possesses some handsome buildings with all modern improvements. The climate is, almost all the year round, like our English summer. After the heat in Australia, which

occasionally reached a hundred degrees in the shade, the cool winds of an Auckland evening were peculiarly refreshing. Orange-trees grow in the orchards, fern-palms in the woods, and flowers of all sorts abound in the gardens. There are now nearly forty thousand inhabitants in the town; and the population is continually increasing.

Not many Maoris are to be seen in the town, but in Auckland there are always a few to be met with, and those we saw interested us greatly. In complexion they are of a rich sienna, with raven-black hair and perfect teeth. The men are of good height, well-proportioned and handsome; the women are not equal to the men, but they are by no means bad-looking. Many are fantastically tattooed across the face, so as to present an almost repulsive appearance. It is remarkable how these Maoris, who are but a colony of Polynesian savages, should have grown to a stature of mind and body in New Zealand which no branch of the race ever attained elsewhere. They are intelligent and learn quickly, and when educated have considerable powers of oratory. There was a time when, within the last half century, missionary platforms rang with the story of the triumphs of the Cross among these dark-skinned Scandinavians of the south. But a cloud came over the sunshine; war between them and the British interfered with the mission work; and the vices of civilisation were introduced. Then followed the Hau-Hau fanaticism, which is a compound of Christianity, Judaism, and heathenism. This, for years, has neutralised the best efforts of the Church. There are signs, however, that once more an effectual door is being opened among them. At an immense gathering held recently in connection with the burial of a prominent chief, our ministers were permitted to conduct religious services. Among those present were many lapsed Wesleyans, including some who had been local preachers. These confessed to the superintendent of our mission that they were weary of wandering from the old faith, and expressed the hope that religious services would once more be held all over what is known as the "king's country." The new king, they thought, would be favourable to such an arrangement. How sad it is that, through contact with the white population, these native races always deteriorate, and their numbers become reduced. With the Maoris there is no exception. They have learned our vices faster than our virtues, and already are being ruined physically, and demoralised in character, by drink.

As our mission in Auckland did not commence until January 20th, we had three weeks for a well-earned rest, part of which we spent in visiting the Maori reserves and the wonderful hot lakes and geysers for which their country is so famous. A railway journey of ten hours took us from Auckland to Rotorua, where the New Zealand wonderland begins. We passed through an open, rolling country with but few traces of cultivation, but with rich undergrowth in the forests, and a dense, unbroken covering of ferns which testified to the richness of the soil, and prophesied of the crops which it will some day produce.

Some new, and often unexpected scene of interest met us at every turn. Of ferns, small and great, there seemed to be no end. In the tree-fern we were particularly interested. Some of these grow to a height of twenty feet; and Nature here is prolific enough to supply the world.

Our excitement was thoroughly aroused as we approached the hot lake district, and saw, for the first time, the columns of vapour rising on every side, and caught whiffs of the sulphur from the boiling springs. The whole district seemed to be on fire. A stay of three days afforded the opportunity of visiting some of the most remarkable scenes. What we saw will be an education, and an experience to be remembered for a lifetime.

We took up our abode at Whakarewarewa, where every variety of geyser and hot spring is within easy access. An intelligent Maori girl, who spoke beautiful English, acted as our guide. She told us she had been educated in a mission-school, where she had been taught to know and love the Saviour. We soon learned that the vapour we had seen on our arrival was steam rising from boiling springs. These were all around us, clear as crystal, and constantly active. The pools are of various capacities, from vast cauldrons capable of boiling an ox, to tiny pools just large enough to cook an egg. The natives cook their fish and boil their potatoes in them. Some serve as washing pools for laundry purposes, and in others, where the water has been tempered by the cold springs, the natives wash themselves. Not having any work to do, they enjoy themselves by spending half their time lounging in the tepid water.

In addition to the pools described, the valley is everywhere perforated with steam holes. Thousands of hissing, spitting, and bubbling jets issue in every direction. Many of these are hidden under dense velvety cushions of beautiful moss. We found the utmost caution needed, lest, by the misplacement of a foot, we should find ourselves unwilling bathers in the boiling waters. Where one day you find firm ground, the next you find a bubbling hole. We walked carefully, as you will imagine, when we realised what a thin crust of earth it was that lay between us and certain death. The geysers were awfully grand. These are energetic, but intermittent. At intervals the water in the crater suddenly becomes agitated, then thousands of large glassy bubbles dance over the surface, and fountains of dazzling brilliance play up to a height of a hundred feet. From some of these a tall, steaming column of water will suddenly shoot into the air, and continue for hours. The water is highly charged with silica. We brought away a small branch of the Ti-tree, which had been left in the water only a week or two, but which now exactly resembles a branch of coral.

Of course we went to the scene of the eruption, where young Bainbridge, of Newcastle, lost his life. A death-like silence reigns supreme where the Maori village lies buried beneath the overwhelming torrent of mud and ashes. The ruins of the Wairoa Hotel give startling evidence of the horrors of the fatal night when the unfortunate victims were killed. The mountain is rent in twain; and, as far as the eye can reach, the whole country is covered with ashes. Nature is doing her best to hide the scene of desolation under a forest of new growth; but it is still a fearful picture of ruin and disaster. The yawning rift in the mountain is still hot and steaming, the stones near its

MAORI GIRLS.

mouth are too hot to handle, and a stick thrust into some of the fissures near the edge will take fire in a moment. An overwhelming sense of the dread majesty of the mighty forces of Nature came upon us as we gazed upon the desolation caused by the eruption, making us painfully conscious of our weakness and insignificance.

Much more we saw, which limited space will not permit us to describe: boiling mud-pools and fountains, lakes of all brilliant colours, close to others dark and muddy, and the home life and customs of the Maoris—all never-to-be-forgotten scenes.

But now about the work of God in the colony. Posters on hoardings and in tramcars, tickets and cards left in all the houses; these, and newspaper advertisements, had, for some weeks, proclaimed that we should begin a mission (D.V.) in the Pitt Street Church, Auckland, on January 20th. The day before the mission commenced, the following interview appeared in the Auckland *Herald*—one of the leading newspapers of the colony. I give it verbatim, because it illustrates how the press helped us in creating interest in the work; and it contains some of my impressions of the colonies:—

"REV. THOMAS COOK'S MISSION

"The Rev. Thomas Cook, the English Wesleyan Conference evangelist, who arrived here last week, commences to-morrow (Sunday) a ten days' mission in Pitt Street Church. As he is a clergyman of note, not only inside his denomination, but out of it, a *Herald* representative interviewed him at his temporary residence, North Shore, where he was enjoying a little rest and retirement, after his evangelistic labours in Australia. Mr. Cook, it may be premised, is in the very prime of life, courteous and genial, and possessed of a well-knit frame. He looks the picture of that health and vigour so necessary for the trying kind of work to which he has devoted himself. Mr. Cook is a native of Yorkshire, and was born at Middlesboro', in 1859, being now in his thirty-sixth year. After the usual preliminaries, the conversation turned to Mr. Cook's mission work.

"EVANGELISTIC OPERATIONS.

"Do you adopt different methods from those of other evangelists?

"My methods differ in many respects from those of other evangelists. The style of preaching is different. I depend upon appealing to the reason, rather than to declamation and dogmatic teaching. I avoid sensationalism and excitement in the meetings. Workers are not permitted to go to the people in the pews and pester them to come into the enquiry-rooms. All who come, come of their own free will. I prefer, also, the enquiry-room to the old-fashioned penitent form. Privacy is thus secured, and the workers are thus better able to deal with the religious difficulties of the seekers. Only picked workers are allowed to engage in this work. My style of preaching is not the old florid style. That style has had its day. Those public teachers who have the largest congregations in England to-day, are the men who talk the ordinary language of daily life—the newspaper English—and avoid the lofty pulpit style. I preach as I talk; and instead of dogmatising offer a personal Saviour to men. I make no attempt to proselytise. My idea is not to promote any particular *ism*, but to promote the Kingdom of our common Master. I solicit, therefore, the co-operation of all Christian people; and as many converts join other churches after my mission as join the Methodist Church. My method differs from that of the Rev. John M'Neill, inasmuch as he does not have after-meetings, but trusts to his discourses and addresses to accomplish the end he has in view. I find after-meetings necessary, in order to guide those who have been impressed and are seeking further counsel. By this means a much larger number are secured to Church membership than would otherwise be the case.

"COLONIAL CHURCH LIFE AND HOME CHURCH LIFE CONTRASTED.

"What phases of colonial Church life strike you as in contrast with home Church life?

"I find the colonies susceptible to religious influence to a much larger extent than I anticipated. I have also been struck with the religious freedom and equality which exist everywhere, and which stand out prominently in contrast with the exclusiveness in many English towns. The various denominations work together better in the colonies, and co-operate more heartily for great public reforms than they do at home. In the colonies there do not seem to be so many men attending church ordinarily as in the mother-country, and the meetings throughout the week are not so well supported and attended. Of course, in London, there is a large non-churchgoing population, which is due to its heterogeneous composition,—a little bit of all the world being put down there,—but London is not England. I am glad to see the temperance movement is taking so large a hold upon the people and upon the churches in the colonies. In England the strides made in that direction are simply marvellous; and the people will scarcely tolerate a clergyman now who is not an abstainer.

"MR. COOK'S IMPRESSIONS OF THE COLONIES.

"What are your impressions of the Australian colonies you have visited?

"I have been so much absorbed in the duties connected with my mission that I have had little time for sight-seeing, or for observing matters outside my religious duties. I noticed a good many ne'er-do-wells and 'remittance men,' who had done no good in the mother country, and have done little better in these new lands when given a fresh chance by their friends. There are to be found in parts of Australia all the extremes of wealth and poverty, which are the blots of the mother country; and the professional beggar is fairly naturalised in some of the colonies. One thing which struck me was the feeling of loyalty everywhere manifested to the mother country, and to the British Government—indeed loyalty to the British Empire is more pronounced in the colonies than at home. Another thing, however, which I noticed in travelling was the lessened respect for authority, and the lessened parental control over the young, which characterise colonial life. This feature bodes danger; for those who grow up heedless of human authority, generally pay little attention to the claims of religion and Divine laws. The season of chastening and depression which the Australian colonies are passing through may possibly teach them to avoid the errors of the past, and to consider more closely the conditions which make for true national progress and prosperity. If so, the lessons of adversity will not have been in vain. I am glad to see that, in the colonies, woman's suffrage is being secured; and it will help the movement at home. Woman's vote will always be cast in the interests of the home, in the interests of morality and religion; and, therefore, no one need fear her having political power. As to climate, I prefer New Zealand to any of the Australian colonies I have visited. The variety of trees to be seen in the landscape is grateful to the eye, after the eternal gum-trees; and the social conditions in this colony are more closely akin to those of English life.

"THE MOTHER COUNTRY AND THE COLONIES.

"Is there any prospect of emigration to these colonies being resumed on a larger scale than of late years?

"The ideas of the mass of the English people about the colonies are still a little hazy; but the English press is gradually enlightening them by devoting greater space to colonial views and colonial affairs. They are also cautious and conservative—largely influenced by traditions—and do not take so readily to new ideas and new ways as colonists. The increase of trade, especially the frozen meat trade, is familiarising the English people with the Australasian colonies; and when they have thoroughly got over their prejudices about frozen meat, a great expansion of that industry may be looked for. Emigration is not likely to be stimulated by the stories of depression which reach them from the colonies; and they think they may as well bear the burdens and struggle for existence in the land of their birth, dear by so many associations, as come out to the colony to undergo the same ordeal and suffering. Besides, within the past ten years a great deal has been done to improve the condition of the working-classes. Hitherto the laws have been made in the interests of capital, now the balance of power is being changed to other hands, and they are being made in the interests of labour. As years roll on, this change will be made more manifest. It is a curious fact, but still a fact, that the most influential of the labour leaders are religious men. The churches are becoming a greater power in politics than they have ever been, and Christians are being taught that politics, in the sense of having the State righteously governed, is a part of religion, and that he is not a good Christian who is not a good citizen, fulfilling all the duties devolving upon him in that position. Never in the history of England have the churches done so much as they are doing to-day to ameliorate the condition of the industrial masses. I may mention that personal friends of my own, Yorkshire manufacturers, are now working their establishments on the co-operative principle, and admitting their men to a share in the profits. By such means they are producing a better feeling between labour and capital, and doing much to prevent strikes.

"THE NEW ZEALAND MISSION OUTLOOK

"In closing the interview, Mr. Cook said: 'I am entering upon the mission in New Zealand with large expectations, having heard of the extensive preparations which have been made, and how earnestly the people are uniting in the matter.'"

When the day arrived for our beginning at Auckland, we soon proved that a great interest had been awakened. Thus, graphically, was the first day of the mission described in the local *Advocate* :—

"The hour of evening service has arrived, and one must be in good time. Rumour says the crowds will be enormous, and an overflow committee has been appointed to hold services in Wesley Hall, if need be. The day has been auspiciously fine. The hot north wind, after breathing stiflingly on the city six weeks, fell on sleep yesterday, and, to-day, the west wind comes freshly up. Pitt Sreet Church is pleasantly cool as we enter it. The westering sun throws his light in floods through the front windows, making the upper parts of the organ glow like fire. Shafts of light fall upon the faces of those seated in the north gallery, and each face that catches the light is radiant. One wonders if there is anything prophetic in it.

"Not yet six o'clock, and the church is more than half full. The streams of incomers are continuous. From this gallery perch one can see nearly all that happens. Home missionaries from the north, and ministers from the Waikato—bidden expressly to the feast—find snug hiding. Edward Best, getting a little deaf now, secures a seat as near the front as possible. After forty years and more of the burden and heat of the day, he longs earnestly to see a great ingathering of souls before he journeys hence. When the mission is over will he be satisfied, I wonder? Not far behind him, serene and thoughtful, sits a man, who, at the last general election, broke a lance with the senior government whip. Has William Shepherd Allen come in from Upper Thames for the pure joy of sharing in the glad excitement of this mission? He has been ever a soul-winner, and he will find the life of the coming week more to his liking than facing flouting foes of the kidney of the member for Parnell.

"Mr. Prior, not once but twice, has to ascend the pulpit, and beseech those who sit in the pews to sit as closely as Christian courtesy dictates. While the choir sing various hymns from the *General Hymnary*, the aisles are seated and filled. The space in and about the communion-rails is blocked; the pulpit-steps and the spare corners flanking the organ will hold no more. It almost looks like a missionary meeting in Oxford Place (Leeds) Chapel.

"Half-past six comes, and with it Thomas Cook. The first impression is favourable. A face not indicative of power and dominant faculty, but fresh and full and smooth. Plenty of head, with the bump of self-esteem cut clean away. Level-headed, one mentally declares, and kindly, and modest, and sympathetic. As he stands, erect, clean-limbed, and fearless, he has the bearing of an uplifted and sanctified son of a Yorkshire dalesman. One feels thankful for the entirely non-professional appearance of the man—hasn't even a shock head of hair to keep ruffling up. Looking at him again, there comes to mind the incident repeated the other day by Mr. Beecroft about Theophilus and Benjamin Gregory visiting George Osborn. 'Did you notice that light on his face?' said the elder brother as they left the house. 'He looks like that in the pulpit.'

"The hymn — from the *General Hymnary* — is announced, and a verse lined out. Quick sympathy is established between the preacher and me, for Thomas Cook sticks to broad, full-vowelled Yorkshire. Ingrained it must be, the result of generations of life among the common people. Joseph Cowen, in the House of Commons, made no effort to rid himself of his Northumbrian burr; Thomas Chalmers thundered in Scottish accents. Why should Thomas Cook chip it, and yah-yah like a Cockney.

"The singing is not quite all one would like. The able and enthusiastic young organist, who has thrown himself heartily into the work of the mission, forgets or ignores the axiom, 'Great bodies move slowly'; and one thought of certain old folk who intensely enjoy congregational singing, but whose wind gives out if the time is undevotionally express. Mr. Burke, swinging his arms, might have been useful. The prayer that follows is simple, quiet, and confident— no passion of pleading, as was the wont of John Rattenbury in his revival days. Rather a statement of desire and preferment of petition, with what seemed like a tacit understanding that what is asked will be granted.

"More singing, and the lesson (Luke xix. from 28th verse to the end of the chapter), with occasional comments. At the conclusion of the lesson Mr. Cook, holding in his hand a few written requests for prayer, asks that many such may be sent in. He also urges the Christians present to make out a list of the names of, say, twelve unconverted friends, and pray that they may be saved during the mission. While all bow in prayer Mr. Cook presents to God the requests handed in.

"Still more singing, and then the congregation settles itself for the sermon. The text is taken from the lesson—41st to 44th verse of Luke xix. The last clause of the 44th verse—'Because thou knewest not the time of thy visitation'—is the burden of the discourse. Lowell's lines—

'Once to every man and nation comes the moment to decide . . .
    Then the choice goes by for ever'

indicates the drift of the sermon. In its logical driving and pinning, it reminded one of the remarkable sermon by H. P. Hughes on the word 'Impossible' (Hebrews vi. 4).

"Telling illustration followed by illustration equally telling, drawn from the preacher's own wide experience, from the life of Darwin, from Drummond, from the destruction of Jerusalem, from physical, organic, and moral law, from Roman history, from stranded wreck and spring tide—all going to show the peril and fatuity of repeatedly rejecting the Christ, and the consequent destruction of receptivity. Warnings were reiterated with terrible emphasis, and, as the sermon progressed, each sentence seemed to make more visible the doom darkening down upon the impenitent. Sometimes the words came in a tumultuous rush, and a pause would ensue, like a mountain torrent steadying itself for another leap.

"The address ended, Mr. Cook desired that every head should be bowed. He then asked those who felt that this was the hour of their visitation to stand up and sit down again. Many did so, as could be inferred from the oft-repeated 'God bless you' of the preacher, and in a brief prayer their desires were laid before God. After another hymn, during which liberty was given to those who wished it to retire, every head was again bowed, and those who had previously stood up were asked to openly and courageously make their way into the enquiry-rooms. While the hymn 'Almost Persuaded' was being softly sung, some rose from their seats and did as they were desired. Between the verses of the hymn, and one or two subsequent hymns, Mr. Cook urged the halting to immediate decision. Avoiding the emotional, he appealed to the best in men—to their sense of right, and to the claims of God to life and service. From thirty to forty eventually went forward, and were received by the large body of willing workers in the class-rooms. With the statement that seventy-five young people had declared their allegiance to Christ at the afternoon service, Mr. Cook closed the meeting. At his request all present gathered in front of the church, and joined in singing, 'All hail the power of Jesus' name.'

"Not in any intellectual power, or any natural gift, or any art, does Mr. Cook's strength lie. He lives in close communion with God, believes in, lives in the enjoyment of, and preaches, entire sanctification, and these stand to the results of his work in the relation of cause to effect."

It would be difficult, even in Leeds, to find more

enthusiasm and spiritual fervour than we found in Auckland. The first Sabbath more than a hundred persons professed to realise God's pardoning mercy. It made one's eyes moist in the afternoon to see bright, intelligent young people—children of the godly and of many prayers—stand up in the crowded congregation, and then bravely make their way down the aisles into the enquiry-rooms. Evening after evening the interest grew, the crowds being great and the number of seekers most gladdening, until about four hundred had professed conversion. The afternoon meetings were times of quiet, melting, yet jubilant, refreshing. Our subject was the complete and joyous conquest of sin through the fulness of the incoming of the Overcomer. The missioner does glory in preaching the majestic truth George Fox emphasised, of the indwelling of God in man. Not a few were helped to claim fulness of blessing in Jesus.

Says one: "I write as a testimony to say that our Father's message by you this week in the afternoon meetings has greatly profited me. *He* has already heard my voice—you, as His servant, will be cheered by my confession, that the joy of His salvation has been—is—restored, and that the blood of Jesus Christ, His son, cleanseth from all sin. Praise the Lord!" "Allow me to thank you," writes Mr. Shepherd Allen, "for the message at Auckland. Not only was it blessed to the conversion of my two lads, but the Sunday morning service was made a great blessing to my own soul. . . ." "I can never be sufficiently thankful," he says, in a later communication, "that my sons and I attended those Auckland services. Both the lads are now on the local preacher's Plan, with several appointments each quarter." It would be impossible to give particular cases of conversion, but I have a heap of letters received from converts telling of new light and power and love. The President of the Conference, who attended most of the meetings, bears testimony as follows:—" The converts that I have seen seem very clear, and are evidently determined to go the whole way. The effect of the mission is, so far, most beneficial to our town, for which we do praise the Lord."

At a praise meeting held the day after we left Auckland, many of the converts witnessed a good confession; and many older Christians told of a decided deepening of spiritual life. "It was a fine sight," writes a minister, "to see the centre of the church filled with people who were all the fruits of the mission. About four hundred names were called over, and three hundred answered to them, and stated what church they wished to join. The great bulk are our own people; but there were some of all sorts, Primitives, Episcopalians, Presbyterians, Baptists, and even a Quaker. Several who could not attend sent very nice letters explaining their absence." "The effect of the mission on the corporate life of the Church will be felt for a long time to come," writes the correspondent of the local religious paper. Several ministers who attended the mission got stirred up and blessed, and at one place, when the minister returned, a revival broke out in which many were converted. He told me, before he left Auckland, that his faith in the old gospel had received a great strengthening, and that he intended to work more on the old-fashioned lines. "I had begun to think," he said, "that the simple preaching of the truth was not sufficient in these days, but what I have seen this week has re-established my confidence." Thus the work went on blessedly sublime. What a mystery of love it is that we should be permitted to be associated with God in His purposes of mercy towards this lost world. We bow humbly at His feet, filled with adoring gratitude, as we record the wonderful blessing He gave with our efforts in Auckland. A large amount of initiatory labour devolved upon the superintendent minister, the Rev. S. F. Prior, and in folding the new converts, which was well and faithfully done. His efficient and cheerful service was greatly appreciated.

From Auckland we went to Wellington, the capital of the colony. Our sail from Onehunga, the port of Auckland, to New Plymouth was anything but pleasant. The wind blew a terrible gale and lashed the sea into fury, even worse than when we came from Sydney. It was bad enough to suffer ourselves, but to be blamed because others suffered was hardly fair, we thought. One, at least, regarded the evangelist as the Jonah of the occasion. When we landed, we went for breakfast to an adjacent hotel, and found there a lady who had been a fellow-passenger. "What a terrible night we have had!" was her greeting. "It has indeed been rough," was our reply. "But I knew we were in for it," she continued; "my friends told me that Evangelist Cook was on board, and I said then we should have a bad time." She must have noticed that my wife and I exchanged glances, because she immediately became confused and stammered awkwardly, "But you are not"— We were obliged to confess who we were, when she relieved herself by saying, "How careful we ought to be!"

The railway journey from New Plymouth to Wellington was painfully tedious, as my readers will believe, when they know that it took fifteen hours to travel two hundred and sixty miles; and ours was the express train. All along the route the forests are being cleared, and small villages are springing up. We saw a number of bush fires, which, at night, were awful in their grandeur. On our arrival at Wellington, the superintendent minister, the Rev. William Baumber and his colleagues welcomed us cordially, and soon made us feel we were among friends again.

Wellington is called the "empire city"; it has a population of about thirty thousand, and a large inter-colonial trade. Many of the streets are very narrow, and the buildings are of wood. Earthquakes have been so severe and so frequent that builders have been afraid to use stone or bricks. The commodious harbour is the most striking feature of the place.

Our services were held in Wesley Church, which will seat a thousand persons, one of the largest buildings in the town. Torrents of rain interfered with the congregations; but we often had the church filled, and always seekers coming forward to enquire of Jesus. But one of the local ministers shall give particulars of the work. He wrote to the *Advocate* as follows:—

"Among the 'memory meetings' held in Wesley Church, may be included the closing meeting of the Rev. Thomas Cook's mission held last evening. The church was crowded—floor, galleries, all. In the front centre seats were gathered a large number of the converts. Old and young were there; some who had been long seeking the Saviour, and others who had been arrested and saved during the mission. The singing was an inspiration, and the address as full of 'points' as the famous Robert Lowe's speeches. It was a happy closing of a most successful mission.

"The attendances were excellent, considering that on the third and fourth evenings—two of the most important—and on the second Sunday, a teeming rain fell. In all the meetings the power of God was present to heal. At the invitation of the preacher the seekers came forward—men, women, and younger people—and went into the enquiry-rooms. There was no excitement, either in church or enquiry-rooms, but a calm, determined deciding for Christ and heaven.

"The hymn-book adopted by Mr. Cook is the *General Hymnary*, the same as is used in Hugh Price Hughes' West End mission work. As may be expected, it is most suitable for such services. The hymns are stronger than Sankey's, though several of Sankey's are included; and they have more spring than many in our Congregational book. And the tunes are well wedded to the words. There is a vitality in the music such as is not found in many of the tunes in our Church book. The singing of 'We're bound for the Land of the pure and the holy,' and the first hymn in the men's meeting, 'Onward, Christian Brothers,' with Mr. Harland at the organ, was a treat to hear. 'It was the hymn that did it,' said one in the enquiry-room, as she referred to a certain hymn sung in one of the services.

That hymn led her to the Saviour. Very thrilling was the singing of 'All hail the power of Jesus' name,' at the close of the service, in the front of the church, by hundreds of people whose hearts had that evening been stirred. On several evenings the hymn was thus sung. The burst of fervent praise made a happy finale to the day.

"Mr. Cook's modes of work are different from those of many who have visited here. He keeps the meeting in his own hands from beginning to end. He is the one influencing agent right through the service. There is no break in the continuity or form. There is no lowering of the tone through some one taking part who is not up to par. And he is well qualified for the work. He is strong, and strength is wanted for such an expenditure of force. His voice is resonant and clear. Without exerting himself in the least, he can be heard all over the large church. He can start a hymn or lead the singing as easily as he can preach. He does not excite himself, though he can catch fire; but the power is in him, and you feel it. The after-meetings, too, are worked differently. Male workers go in with men who are enquirers, and female workers with women. These workers are chosen members of the church, with special qualifications for the work. They are adorned with a rosette, the aim being to prevent undesirable workers from entering the rooms. At the close of the service Mr. Cook goes into the enquiry-rooms, and after addressing and shaking hands with those who have found peace, deals personally with those who are still in difficulty. A card, containing 'Helps to Seekers,' is given to each enquirer. This has aided many in their holy quest.

Very firm is he in requiring that every one should intelligently and clearly grasp the Lord Jesus as a Saviour. The modes of work are different, but they are successful—successful in winning men to the Lord, not in the weakness of excitement, but in the strength of deliberate choice. After seeing the thoroughness of the work done, one feels confident in predicting that much of the fruit will remain.

"The afternoon meetings for the deepening of the spiritual life were most helpful. Very clearly were the Christian's privileges shown. The sanctified life, not an unsinning state, but an unsinning condition through a moment-by-moment obedience and trust, was understood and entered into by many as it had not been before. Prejudices against that life, caused by the wild statements and censoriousness of professors, were removed. The difference between blamelessness and faultlessness was clearly apprehended; and a fuller surrender made, that the blameless life on earth and the faultless life of heaven might be enjoyed. There was no after-meeting of seekers; but many of God's people as they heard the message, the eyes of their understanding being opened, perceived and received in Christ a fuller blessing.

"The results of the mission have been most encouraging. The rally of the members, and they have rallied round their minister well, has bound them to the Church with a closer, stronger bond. God's people have taken a higher stand, and some two hundred and thirty have professed conversion. These have been members of different congregations, including Roman Catholic. Over one hundred belonged to Wesley Church, or have expressed a wish to join that

Church. 'I'm as happy as you are now,' said an old man to Mr. Baumber at the close of the mission. At the early part he was not happy, for the weight of a life of sin was upon him; but that weight had been removed, and hence his joy. But all were happy; and in last night's songs of praise this happiness was shown. Our mouths are filled with singing, and our hearts with love and thankfulness!"

"And the work goes on," writes another correspondent; "four were brought to God last Sunday, and four others the Sunday before. So it spreads and grows."

In my appeals to young men I made a strong point of the importance of saving our lives as well as our souls. "God cannot make not to have been, what has been"; and if we lose the best years of our life, the loss can never be retrieved. Throughout eternity we shall suffer, even if we are forgiven, because our reward will be less than it would have been had we given God the years that were wasted. Besides, the possibilities of service become smaller as we grow older; the clay becomes "marred in the hands of the Potter," and after each lost year the vessel that is made of it is inferior in quality compared with what it would have been the previous year. Even God cannot make as much of a life dedicated to Him at the age of twenty-five, as He could have done with that same life, if it had been given to Him in its youth. It was this sort of appeal at Wellington that brought the following response:—"Much of your address last evening touched me deeply, especially the reference to the clay marred in the hands of the Potter. The writer was a happy worker in connection with one of your earlier missions, and should have been now in the ranks of the ministry; but, wickedly choosing another path for himself, has lost these many years of possible usefulness, for which he has been justly punished in many ways, but in none so severely as in the torments of remorse. Do you think that even at this late hour there is a possibility of this terribly marred clay being fashioned into some vessel of usefulness? I am bitterly conscious that it can never be now what it was intended to be, but I am willing to have it made whatever is still possible. Please pray the great Potter to give it another turn; and warn the young men especially against wilful disregard of the Divine call." Would that young men would learn the lesson, that they will never be worth as much to God again as they are now. Every year lost interferes with God's purpose concerning their life. God may forgive them later, but the work they can do for Him is less and less valuable the longer they postpone their decision to serve Him. God must have our whole life at His disposal, otherwise He can never get out of our life all that was possible. Says Dr. Miller: "Human life must appear very pathetic, and ofttimes tragical, as the angels look down upon it. There are almost infinitely fewer wrecks on the great sea where the ships go, than on the other sea of which poets write, where lives with their freightage of immortal hopes and possibilities sail on to their destiny." Life is given to us as a prey. We may crown it with blessing, or poison it with anguish. If we fritter away and waste it, we shall not have another wherewith to try and redeem its unutterable loss. One trial alone shall we have—

only one life to make or to mar. How important, then, that we should be wise in time, not only to avoid the follies that have marred and stained the lives of others, but to make the best of ourselves before the doors of our opportunities are closed.

> "Life is a leaf of paper white,
> Whereon each one of us may write
> His word or two—and then comes night."

REV. WILLIAM MORLEY.
REV. C. E. BEECROFT.   REV. T. F. PRIOR.

CHAPTER IX

NEW ZEALAND

Christchurch—Timaru—Dunedin—New Plymouth

WE are all agreed that conversion, which is the chief aim of the evangelist, is not the ultimate end of preaching. Conversion is the beginning of the work, when the convert becomes a scholar who is just starting to learn. Christian life must ripen, and knowledge and character must be cultivated. The pastor and teacher are as necessary, therefore, as the evangelist — the one is but the complement of the other. Each must be careful not to discredit the other. The Church needs both, or her work will be onesided, distorted, and disappointing. Some pastors have hesitated about inviting evangelists to assist them in reaping their harvests, because they have thought that importing outside help tends to belittle and disparage the installed shepherds of the flock. The result has often been that their opportunity has been allowed to pass; the harvest which was ready has rotted; those who might then have been easily won for Christ have broken away never to be recovered to the Church. What are the successes of the evangelist but the successes of patient labourers, many and varied, who have preceded them! Our success means the success of ministers, teachers, parents, and the personal efforts of all classes of Christians. Revivals, to be genuine and permanent, are scarcely possible unless they have been prepared for by much sowing and watering, and the prayers of the saints. And after our missions are ended, unless the converts are watched over and cared for, our work is in vain. Some have said "it is a thankless task to watch over another man's converts." But is it not possible that those who have preceded and followed the evangelist will have done more towards winning these souls for Christ than the evangelist whose converts they are said to be? The great difficulty to-day is not to win men for Christ, but to keep in the faith those won for Him. The responsibility of the under-shepherds needs to be emphasized, and the need there is of organisation whereby each convert shall receive personal attention and help. To this end the ministers in the colonies, at the places we visited, formed vigilance bands, each member of which undertook to look after two or three of those who had professed decision for Christ, for six months, visiting them each week, and at a monthly meeting reporting progress. By this means a very large proportion of the enquirers was retained by the churches.

After ten days in Wellington we moved on to Christchurch, where we found Methodism strong and well represented. Christchurch is the most English town in the whole colony. It is popularly known as the "city of the plains," and has a population of thirty thousand. Situated on the banks of the Avon, which winds about through the town, it reminds one of our university towns, such as Cambridge. Its streets are wide and regular, and the buildings such as would do credit to our largest provincial towns. The museum—one of the finest in the colonies—was a great attraction. It was there we saw several skeletons of the giant extinct bird, the moa, which was formerly indigenous to New Zealand. The skeletons must have been sixteen feet in height. Even the traditions of the natives fail to give any satisfactory account of this ornithological wonder, which is now only known by its bones found in the caves where they have lain for ages protected from the disintegrating effects of the weather. The following description will be read with interest:—

"What Niagara is to ordinary waterfalls, the moa was to the bird tribe. It belonged to the Titans which dwelt upon the earth in the days of the dodo and the mastodon. . . . It was a long time before the incredulous naturalists could be induced to admit of the possible existence of such a gigantic bird on the earth's surface at any period of the globe's history. Of late years, however, several enterprising naturalists have made trips to New Zealand from both Europe and America, for the sole purpose of examining and reporting upon that marvellous skeleton."

The country surrounding Christchurch, known as the Canterbury Plains, comprises what is perhaps the richest and most fully developed land in New Zealand.

During the ten years previous to our visit the people of Christchurch had had such ample cause to look askance at many of the self-styled evangelists who had visited them, and had been, withal, so cursed by a pseudo-evangelism, that some of the most earnest of our well-wishers felt that, in their city, we should have harder ground to break than in any other part of New Zealand. But, from the very outset, God distinctly put His seal upon our work. There were few, if any, dry eyes during the first service. Prejudices were swept away, and certain fastidious members of the congregation, who were inclined to fear lest noise and rant should be characteristics of the mission, were reassured. All felt the mighty power of God. At each of the three services on the first Sabbath, the great building was crowded, and at the close of the day from fifty to sixty had professed to find peace with God. Throughout the week the mission grew in interest and intensity. Night after night the church was thronged with eager, earnest listeners. Nothing was more noticeable than the large number of men—men of all ranks and social grades in the community — who attended the services. Indeed, one of the most hopeful and inspiring sights of the whole mission was witnessed on the Friday evening, when we held our service for men only. Referring to this service, a local paper justly observed: " Truly, Christianity is not played out yet. Society has not finally broken with Christ, or it would be impossible to crowd one of the largest churches in New Zealand, on a week night, with men manifestly eager to drink in the story, old, but ever new, ' of Jesus and His love.' If the mission had pointed no other lesson than this, it would not have been in vain : that the old truths still hold potent sway over the hearts of men ; that in the wistful eyes of the world there is still a longing after God, and a hunger at its heart for His righteousness and rest."

The mission, which lasted ten days, closed on the second Tuesday night, when hundreds were unable to obtain admission. The converts, numbering about three hundred, that night occupied the middle portion of the church, thus publicly testifying that they had decided for Christ. But the results, even as regards converts, will never be tabulated. Eternity alone will reveal them. Some, we have heard of since, found pardon in their pews under the preaching of the Word, and others in the privacy of their own homes. A most striking feature was the large proportion of elderly people among the enquirers. At the praise-meeting, one old man, white with the frosts of seventy winters—long enslaved by the drink curse—spoke in tremulous tones of God's great mercy to him, and of how, for the first time for many years, he had now a happy home. A Scotchwoman, who had come many miles "on purpose to get converted," as she put it, called forth shouts of praise as she told of the new gladness that had come to her heart.

Of the converts' service held after the mission, the minister writes: "We had a magnificent meeting. Between two and three hundred of the converts were present. Many wrote expressing regret that they could not attend. Considerably over two hundred will join our church; the balance will join other churches. It has been a blessed time for us, and will make an era in the history of the Church. There has been nothing like it since that never-to-be-forgotten time when 'Californian' Taylor conducted a similar mission here. The whole Church has been lifted up, and the members fired with a new zeal. Last Sabbath we held the sacrament of the Lord's Supper both morning and evening, and such a season we have never had in my memory."

On the second Sunday morning I preached on "Prevailing prayer, and how to offer it." At the close of the service, a minister who was present told me that he had attended a mission I conducted in England—at Walsall—several years before, when he asked for prayer on behalf of two friends who were sick and unconverted. Within three months both were rejoicing in Christ as their personal Saviour, and have since died triumphantly in the Lord. Glad enough were we to find, also, that work done for Christ in England bears fruit yonder. In almost every town we visited, my heart was thrilled with the remark, "You led me to Christ in the old country," and this testimony from one of the ministers at Christchurch was especially encouraging. He had been converted in a mission I held at Truro in 1885.

The converts were of all conditions and ages. What pathetic scenes we witnessed! The embracings of husbands and wives, of brothers and sisters, parents and children, teachers and scholars. A wife was brought by her husband, who had been saved the previous night, and would not sleep until she promised to come with him on the morrow. "I promised a dying sister that I would meet her in heaven, and this is the fulfilment of the promise," said a big manly fellow, as he fell on his knees in the enquiry-room and cried, "God be merciful to me a sinner!" An elderly man, who had found the peace that "passeth understanding," told me his heart had been so broken the previous night that in bed he could not sleep for weeping, and found no rest until he pledged himself to confess Christ. God met him almost as soon as he entered the room. These are records from my diary of one night among the enquirers. "So mightily grew the Word of God and prevailed."

While in Christchurch we made the acquaintance of the Rev. William Morley. He was, at that time, President of the Australasian General Conference, and Connexional Secretary of New Zealand. Under his wise and energetic administration the home missions of the colony have become a great force. Mr. Morley's career has been eminently distinguished. Twice he has been called to the chair of the New Zealand Conference, and four times elected to the secretaryship. As editor of the *New Zealand Wesleyan*, and principal of Three Kings' College, as well as in Circuit work, he has served the Church faithfully and well. To his other qualities must be added that of intense spiritual fervour. His prayers during our mission were remarkable for unction and power; and at the Conference a few weeks later, several penitents came forward to seek salvation after his sermon. By his kindliness of manner and brotherly sympathy with our work, Mr. Morley completely won our affection and esteem. Of the Rev. H. R. Dewsbury, also, we cherish grateful remembrances, not only for preparing our way so thoroughly, but for the generous hospitality which he and Mrs. Dewsbury provided for us. The joy of making so many new and real friends was, in itself, ample reward for any inconveniences we suffered during our tour. There are no friendships so warm and lasting as those made during a revival.

At Timaru, our next place of labour, the Rev. C. E. Beecroft was superintendent minister. We had known Mr. Beecroft in England, and were delighted to renew the friendship. His friends in England will be pleased to learn how richly God blessed his Circuit.

Timaru is a seaport in the centre of the richest agricultural district in the Middle Island. There are mills for grinding flour, for making cloth, and for preparing woodwork. The place is thriving, and has a still better prospect. The population is between four and five thousand. During our visit the Rev. Joseph Olphert, from England, was Mr. Beecroft's guest, and rendered valuable service to the mission. It was quite cheering to have him with us. Home seemed so much nearer because of his presence, and the home news he brought was most welcome. Concerning the mission, Mr. Beecroft wrote so forcefully to the *Advocate* that I cannot do better than reproduce his articles:—

"'We *always* turn up,' was Thomas Cook's cheery greeting at Timaru, on the afternoon of March 1st. There had been a momentary sense of disappointment. The welcoming party had looked for him at the wrong end of the train, and it was a relief to hear the ringing voice, 'All right: here we are!'

"As many readers of the *Advocate* know by this time, the 'we' applies to a genuinely happy pair, who, in successful service for the Master, must surely be tasting as fully of the cup of satisfaction as any two Christians in New Zealand just now. The missioner looks, if anything, younger than when the writer used to meet him at the London Ministers' Meetings eight years ago. His clear, open countenance has the glow of health upon it. Better still, it is radiant with what his namesake of the Boston Temple calls 'the solar look.' With a justifiable pride, he hastens to say of the sweet-faced lady at his side, 'This is my wife'; and in a few moments they are away to the quiet home circle in which they will be welcome guests during their stay in Timaru.

"Mr. Cook's previous missions have been conducted in the midst of large populations, and in the centres of Methodist influence. It was, therefore, not without a sense of responsibility that this Circuit presented its request for a visit from the evangelist. But though not numerically strong in proportion to the population, it was felt that our Church ought to embrace the opportunity for effort and blessing. And already, though the mission is not much more than half over, our hearts are filled with rejoicing, and our lips with thanksgiving.

"Without any design on the part of our Anglican friends, the visit of the Bishop of Melanesia, with his twenty native converts, coincided with the opening Sunday and Monday of the mission. Notwithstanding this strong counter-attraction, the Bank Street Church was comfortably filled at the morning service. It was evident, from the outset, that One who had said, 'Go in this thy might,' had looked upon the preacher. The opening prayer was that of a man who knew the way to the throne. 'Thou hast given Thy servant credentials,' he pleaded; 'let it be seen that Thou art with him; and let a great hush come upon the people because God is in the midst.'

"To a preacher who was rehearsing the Divine attributes in laboured phrases a simple Methodist once gave the open counsel, 'Call Him Father, and ask

Him for something.' That is what Thomas Cook does; and his fellow-worshippers know that the Father heareth.

"The preacher's style and manner have been already fully described. There is no mistaking the meaning of his terse, incisive sentences. They have not been shaped to please the ear, but to convince the judgment, to move the will, and to reach the heart of the hearer. His aim is not to be admired by, but to be 'understanded of, the people.' Whilst disclaiming greatness, he unconsciously achieves it—the greatness of simplicity.

"When King George III., of England, listened to a plain gospel sermon, he would say to the pew-opener as he passed out of the church, 'That will do; that will feed souls.' All Thomas Cook's sermons are of this nutritious order. He is emphatically what Cuyler calls 'a vigorous, meaty, instructive preacher.' Those who have, themselves, been engaged for years in the endeavour to apply and illustrate the Word of God, have had cause to admire and rejoice in the evangelist's skill in 'opening and alleging' the truths of the gospel. Following the apostolic method, he expounds and testifies, before he seeks to persuade men, concerning Jesus. A singularly accurate exegesis of his text is illumined by choicest illustration, drawn from a wide range of reading, and enriched by incident from his store of hallowed memories. Like Charles Haddon Spurgeon, he occasionally introduces the testimony of personal experience with marked effect. He is no theoriser, or recounter of other men's opinions, but himself believes, and therefore speaks. So, to use his own words, he does not use the pulpit as 'an agitation desk, but as a witness box.' He has no doubt to air, but a living and joyous conviction to proclaim.

"At the Saturday afternoon service senior scholars from the Presbyterian, Baptist, and Primitive Methodist Churches were present by invitation, accompanied by their teachers. Nearly fifty young people, representing each of these schools, entered the enquiry-rooms, and most of them were enabled, before leaving, to rejoice in the Saviour. The Rev. Joseph Olphert, of the English Conference, took charge of this after-meeting, in the absence of Mr. Beecroft at a country appointment.

"In the evening the strong voice of the preacher rose above the noise of the ceaseless downpour on the roof of the church. The power of God was manifestly present as he set forth the solemn consequences of neglecting the day of visitation.

"A lantern lecture at the theatre, by the Melanesian bishop, thinned the Monday night's attendance; but on each succeeding evening the church has been filled, and seats have been required in the aisles. The afternoon meetings, for the deepening of the spiritual life, have been seasons of singular profit and blessing— and have been attended by the ministers and members of the churches in the town. Up to Thursday evening one hundred and eleven enquirers have professed faith in Christ. These include men and women above forty years of age, and many of our own young people.

"The second Sunday of Mr. Cook's mission in Timaru answered to the good old George Herbert's description—

> 'Sweet day, so cool, so calm, so bright,
> The bridal of the earth and sky.'

"After a spell of north-westerly winds, with their accompaniments of heat and driving dust, a morning without clouds ushered in an ideal Sabbath, in which a welcome quiet rested on land and sea. The refreshing outward influences were reflected in the experience of each service of the day. More than sixty were present at the early prayer-meeting. The Rev. W. Gillies, of the Presbyterian Church, who had discovered at Mr. Cook's week-day meetings that he himself had 'been a Methodist for years,' was again with us. Several of the converts offered brief prayers, and the hearts of elder Christians were stirred by memories of their own early joy in God, as these new voices, trembling with emotion, were heard for the first time in public petition.

"Every pew and chair was occupied at the morning service, when Mr. Cook preached on the subject of 'Prevailing Prayer.' 'Where have we been living,' said one of our members, afterwards, 'that we have asked so little, and might have had so much?' The congregation at the afternoon meeting was a sight to see. Pews, aisles, choir seats, and vestries were filled with men. Such a gathering at a religious service was probably never seen in Timaru before. There was a little shyness at the singing of the first hymn; but after the prayer and a few sentences of welcome from Mr. Cook, all reserve was dispelled. The audience evidently surrendered itself to a recognised leader. At the second hymn—'Stand up, stand up for Jesus'—there was a magnificent roll of harmony. During the delivery of the sermon on the 'Unalterable consequences of conduct,' the 'hush' for which the preacher had prayed at the outset of the mission rested on the whole congregation. Eighteen youths and men went into the enquiry-room, and some of the workers found their 'prayer lists' getting wonderfully shortened. The majority of those who there and then found the Saviour were members of our own congregations in town or country; but once more our Presbyterian friends shared with us in the joy of the harvest.

"It is on record that, one morning, the deacons of Park Street Chapel found all the windows broken on one side of the building, and, though Mr. Spurgeon suggested a reward of five pounds for the discovery of the offender, they gravely shook their heads. The pastor's own walking-stick was believed to have been concerned in the mischief. History repeats itself. The packed congregation at Timaru, on the evening of the 10th, finding the atmosphere of the church less like that of the Black Hole of Calcutta than they had feared it would be, noted with thankfulness that many of the upper panes of glass were missing. Some peculiar scratches are, at present, visible on the handle of a staff that was in the minister's possession that afternoon. Though every available place within the church was occupied, numbers had to go away. Seats were arranged on the slope outside the building, and as the darkness deepened without, the light from the open door fell upon a group of eager faces turned towards the preacher. The workers in the enquiry-rooms were again provided with congenial employment at the after-meeting.

"The closing service of the mission was held on Tuesday evening in the Presbyterian Church, which was crowded to its utmost capacity before the time for commencing. Besides the ministers of the town, the Revs. J. J. Doke, of Christchurch, C. Abernethy, and C. H. Standage gave willing help in the enquiry-room, and nearly forty seekers professed faith in Christ. The total number of enquirers in Timaru has been two hundred and twenty; and we fervently trust that the end is not yet.

"On Wednesday evening a praise and testimony meeting was held in our own church, presided over by the Rev. C. E. Beecroft, accompanied by the Revs. W. Gillies and C. Abernethy. Converts had come in from Temuka and all the country places in the Timaru Circuit. For nearly two hours the quickened members of the Church and the newly-saved united in witness and thanksgiving, a very sacred influence resting on all. At the close four more seekers entered into the liberty of the children of God.

"It is but one short fortnight since we welcomed Mr. and Mrs. Cook amongst us. Now they are away —followed by the prayer and loving regard of all who have come to know them. Mrs. Cook's unobtrusive service in the enquiry-room has been valuable alike to co-workers and seekers, and her name will be gratefully associated with that of her husband in all remembrances of the mission.

"A mark has been set upon the life of the Wesleyan Church in Timaru, which will be visible for long years to come, whilst the wider influence that has been brought into exercise is altogether beyond our power to estimate. Only the Day will declare it.

"We unite with Mr. Cook in looking beyond the instrumentality to the great Source of blessing, and render thanks and praise to Him who 'when He led captivity captive, and gave gifts unto men . . . gave some evangelists . . . for the edifying of the body of Christ.'"

As elsewhere, so at Timaru, the mission furnished illustrations of the surprises of grace. Amongst these was a remarkable fulfilment of the words: "I am sought of them that asked not for me; I am found of them that sought me not." A man in mid-life, who had heard nothing whatever of the mission, rode over on his bicycle from Temuka, a town twelve miles distant, on the afternoon of the second Sunday, intending to see a local tradesman on business. Instead of asking for Mr. John —— he asked for Mr. J——, and was directed to the house of Mr. James ——, the brother of the person he was seeking. This friend had just returned from the men's meeting, and pressed his unexpected visitor to stay tea and go with him to the evening service. The Word reached his heart, and he was found among the seekers at the after-meeting. The business that had brought him into town was forgotten in "the great transaction." He "left caring for" the iron in the search for the pearl of great price, and rode home that night in the moonlight filled with adoring love to God.

Along that same road, that same evening, a Circuit steward and his wife were returning with the son in whose conversion the prayers and hopes of years had been fulfilled. The young man, writing to his minister a few days afterwards, said: "I had been trying to get saved for about two years. I thought it would be impossible for me to give up all my bad habits at once, so I tried to break them off one at a time; and the more I tried the worse I got, till Sunday week, at the meeting for men only, God showed me plainly that the only way I could get saved was by trusting in Him." Another of the converts was the secretary of the Sunday school. His irreproachable character, genial disposition, and promising gifts had won the esteem of all about him. Only one thing was lacking, personal consecration to Christ. He had been an attendant on Church of England services in his boyhood. Our methods were, therefore, entirely new to him; and he resented what he considered the drawing of attention to himself, when he had to remain seated whilst those who had decided for God were asked to stand up. For several days he absented himself from the mission, but was persuaded to attend the service for men only. To the joy of all the workers, he was the first to enter the enquiry-room, where, disclaiming his own righteousness, he became heir of "the righteousnees which is of God by faith."

Throughout the whole mission the Rev. W. Gillies, the Presbyterian minister, entered most heartily into the work, with the result that he had the joy of seeing nearly all the members of the Bible class brought to Christ, together with several adult members of his congregation. One man who found peace on a Tuesday evening, went, the next morning before nine o'clock, to the manse to tell his minister, and the following evening walked out six miles to let his own brother know that he had made "the great choice." Similar testimonies might be multiplied, but these must suffice. Writing later, Mr. Beecroft says: "The work here is not at an end. We have to rejoice that burdened souls are still coming to the gracious

Shepherd. . . . After allowing for those who were already on the roll of membership, but who had come out into a clearer sense of acceptance with God, I had the privilege of announcing, to the quarterly meeting last night, that one hundred and one names had been placed 'on trial.' It is not surprising that our meeting proved one of the most harmonious and hopeful in the memory of its members." Of a truth the reaper overtook the sower, but both rejoiced together. In Mr. Beecroft we hardly knew which we admired most, his toilsome self-denying labour, or his genial brotherliness and saintly character. We do not wonder at the respect and esteem in which he is held by his people. Our fellowship with him is one of the most pleasant memories we have of New Zealand.

From Timaru we went to Dunedin, where we arrived on Friday, March 15th. Our mission commenced on the Sabbath. Dunedin is the capital of Otago, and is admittedly the finest built city in New Zealand. It takes high rank in commercial importance, having at its back a magnificent agricultural, pastoral, and mining country, and contains extensive woollen, iron, leather, and other factories. The population, with suburbs, is upwards of five thousand, the majority of the people being of Scotch extraction. This is attributable to the fact that the colonisation of Otago was controlled by a "lay association" of the Free Church of Scotland. The first settlers arrived in the ship *John Wycliffe* in the year 1848, which was followed within a month by the *Philip Laing*. Twelve months later the population was computed to consist of seven hundred and forty-three persons, which increased the following year to eleven hundred and eighty-two. After that the population increased by leaps and bounds. The people retain all their national characteristics, being plodding and persevering, as well as self-reliant and hopeful. The attachment to their Church is evidenced by the handsome ecclesiastical buildings they have erected. Some are noble specimens of architecture. We had feared lest bigotry and exclusiveness might obtain; but instead of that the various churches worked with us in Dunedin with a heartiness and catholicity such as we have never met with before.

The arrangements for the mission were all we could wish. The Garrison Hall had been chosen for the *locale* of the services; and the most was made of the accommodation the hall affords. Special staging had been erected for the convenience of the choir, which consisted of at least one hundred and fifty voices. More than two thousand persons were provided for; but even this accommodation was insufficient. On the first Sunday evening, long before the time of service, all seats were occupied, and numbers had to be turned away. Between thirteen and fourteen hundred attended the men's meeting on the Friday evening. Such a congregation on a pouring wet night indicated the extent of the interest awakened. One of the local papers described that service as "unique in the history of the colony." The second Sabbath was, as usual, "the great day of the feast." At the four meetings held that day more than seven thousand persons were present. Although the services during the earlier part of the mission were accompanied with every sign of success, the result of the last three days was especially noteworthy. It was estimated that nearly thirteen thousand attended during those days, while one hundred and forty-three professed conversion, and the offertories realised ninety-five pounds sterling. Altogether, during the mission three hundred and eight gave their names in the enquiry-rooms as having decided for Christ; but many others have been heard of since who did not make a public confession. All sections of the Church will receive increase. In other towns our missions were held in Wesleyan churches, but in Dunedin, the fact of the services being held in a hall made the platform broader, and other churches beside our own shared largely in the blessing.

In both Australia and New Zealand we found the utmost harmony and good feeling existed between the various churches, and a much greater readiness to unite for evangelistic effort than prevails among the churches at home. From the results which attended such united meetings wherever we held them, I am led to the firm conviction that in such union we have one of the most valuable agencies that can be employed to promote a general advance of the Kingdom of Christ. One may "chase a thousand" but *two* shall "put ten thousand to flight." Our home at Dunedin was with the Rev. J. J. and Mrs. Lewis. Mr. Lewis has occupied some of the best Circuits in the colony. He is a scholarly and thoughtful preacher, with a loving, Christian spirit. While strictly adhering to the good old Methodist doctrines and usages, he is of liberal views, and has helped much in securing the extension of the ministerial term, and Methodist union. He strongly advocates the doctrine of Christian perfection, which truth he has helped to keep disentangled from misrepresentation. In 1890

Mr. Lewis was elected to the chair of the Conference. Methodism in New Zealand is of a very active and advanced type, and few have helped more to make it what it is than Mr. Lewis. After we left Dunedin, Mr. Lewis sent us details of several most interesting conversions which had taken place during the mission. Lack of space compels the omission of some, but to a few I may be allowed to advert.

On the day following the close of the mission a vessel sailed from Dunedin, having on board ten Christian sailors. Nine of these had been converted during the mission. A well-known business man,—a trustee of one of our suburban churches,—and universally respected for his sterling integrity, was, yet, a stranger to experimental religion. His parents had been, for many years, prominent and consistent members of the Wesleyan Church, and the son had been the subject of many prayers. He was drawn to attend the mission; and, one night, in a powerful service, publicly confessed himself a seeker of salvation. Though he entered the enquiry-room, he did not there find the blessing he sought; but when at home, after a long and severe struggle, the light came, and at the thanksgiving service he rose to testify that he knew Christ as his personal Saviour. Another man travelled nearly a hundred miles to attend the services, hoping to meet with the Saviour whom he had been seeking for some time. He went home rejoicing in the "indubitable witness" of the Divine favour. The Pelichet Bay Mission had been the most needy, yet disheartening, part of the Circuit extension. The "larikin" element had, at times, been so wild as almost to break up the service. The workers of the mission were overjoyed when the most unmanageable of the "larikins" came out among the enquirers in response to my invitation. Some were sceptical concerning the genuineness of the work, but the change in the youth is now evident to all. Nor did the work cease with our leaving. On the following Sabbath, the superintendent minister reports, "several conversions and almost doubled collections"; and still later the secretary writes: "Souls are being brought to God in almost every Sunday service. I have heard of no falling away among the converts. Some are already engaged in active work for the Master."

A word of praise is due to the choir for the very excellent service they rendered. The singing of more than a hundred trained voices helped much to maintain interest in the mission. There was also a large number of persons who gave assistance as ushers and attendants, whilst Mr. Rosevear, as secretary, was the embodiment of business tact combined with Christian courtesy. He rendered invaluable service. Not in any human power were these victories won. The editor of the Presbyterian *Outlook* expressed the truth exactly when he said: "There is nothing either in Mr. Cook's matter or manner to account for it. There is no explanation of it short of the Holy Spirit." Mr. Moody was right when he called the Holy Ghost the "One Great Revivalist."

We shall not soon forget the affectionate farewell and good wishes of the little crowd that gathered at the station as we left. Our destination was Oamaru, where we had promised to spend two days on our way to New Plymouth. The six hours' journey was pleasantly broken at Timaru, where, at the station, quite a host of our friends had assembled to wish us God-speed. "Our Church is transformed," was the universal testimony; "and we mean to keep the work going," shouted some of the more enthusiastic ones as our train left the platform.

Our great regret at Oamaru was, that our stay was necessarily so brief. We made the best, however, of the time at our disposal. All the churches joined in the movement; and on the Sabbath the Baptists, Congregationalists, and Salvation Army gave up their evening service and came to our assistance. We held six services during the two days, with the result that about eighty persons professed conversion. This, in a small town of not more than five thousand inhabitants, produced a deep impression. The ministers of the several churches decided to continue the services.

Only those who have travelled in the colonies can form a correct estimate of the peculiar adaptation of the Wesleyan Methodist Church system to meet the pressing needs of these new countries, with their large, widespread, and rapidly increasing populations. Our New Zealand Church is especially vigorous. The ratio of denominational growth since 1886 has been as follows:—Roman Catholic, 8·12; Presbyterian, 8·29; Episcopalian, 9·02; Methodist, 14·61. Our ministers, generally, are aggressive and spiritual, and of liberal and advanced views. It was the New Zealand Conference that first decided upon the extension of the ministerial term in a Circuit; and they have also led the way in Methodist union. A policy of this active and advanced type is necessary to keep pace with the progress of the colony. The women's franchise has done much to promote the interests of temperance and morality. Prohibition is, at last, within measurable distance. In all social reform the colony is in advance of the other colonies, and far ahead of England. Of course, mistakes are made by both government and church; but these will be rectified after experience. The giving up of the class-meeting as a test of Church membership has been a great blunder. The ministers are almost unanimous in this confession. The monthly meeting has proved a wretched substitute. In this particular I advised a return to the "old paths"; and not a few promised to do their best to forward it.

Our last mission in New Zealand was one of the best. It was held at New Plymouth, the chief town of the Taranaki province in North Island, and under the shadow of Mount Egmont. The district around was the scene of the greatest difficulties with the Maoris; but now it is among the best cultivated land of the colony. The population of the town does not exceed five thousand; but the influence of the mission was felt throughout the entire province, as will be seen from the addresses of the converts. Names were taken, in the enquiry-room, of persons from Okato, eighteen miles distant; Mangorei, six miles; Pungarehu, twenty-seven miles; Lepperton and Egmont, eight miles; Tikorangi, fourteen miles; Waitara, ten miles; Eltham, forty miles; Inglewood, twelve miles; and even Lyttleton and Onehunga. At almost every service hearers from adjoining Circuits, who had come in brakes, buggies, and every kind of conveyance, were present by scores. A

Sunday-school teacher brought his class eighteen miles to hear the message, and had the joy of witnessing several of them decide to serve the Lord. On the first Sabbath, no less than eighty professed decision for Christ. "Bless God," said a venerable brother with moistened eye, "I put twelve names on my prayer list, and three have been converted the first day." Night by night during the week, we rejoiced over enlarged congregations and increased seriousness, until the mission became the topic of conversation everywhere. Even the local paper testified: "A great impression has undoubtedly been made upon the whole district." On the second Monday, so inclement were the elements, that a ball, largely advertised and popular, had to be postponed; but between four and five hundred came to hear the Word of Life, and a goodly number resolved henceforth to be the Lord's. At a women's meeting an old lady, eighty-four years of age, found salvation. Her daughter came to decision at the same service, giving as her reason: "Three of my children have been converted, and I must not be left behind." Several elderly men were among the seekers, one of whom had been a freethinker for thirty years.

One case illustrates the working of the law of conscience. God has so constituted our nature that it is impossible for a man not to suffer the keenest agony when the naked fact of his guilt is laid upon his conscience by the Spirit of God, and held there. The fear of detection is always, more or less, painfully felt. Speaking of this, I told the story of a burglar who entered and rifled the contents of an unoccupied dwelling. He ransacked the rooms, from attic to cellar, and heaped his plunder together in the parlour. There were evidences that there he had sat down to rest, perhaps to think. On a bracket in a corner stood a marble bust of Guido's Ecce Homo—Christ crowned with thorns. The guilty man had taken it in his hands and examined it,—it bore the marks of his fingers,—but he had replaced it, and turned its face to the wall, as if he would not have even the cold, sightless eyes of the marble Saviour look upon his deed of infamy. In application, I asked, "Is it not an instinct of human nature to want to hide its sin from those of purer eyes. How will it be then when we have to face the living Christ, and He looks us through and through with His eyes of flame?" This was on the Wednesday night of the first week. On the following Tuesday one of the seekers was unusually broken down and penitent, and told us, afterwards, how he had suffered awful torture since he heard the story of the burglar. "That eye," he said, "has followed me ever since, and I have not been able to get away from it. It has haunted me night and day."

These are a few specimen cases from the two hundred and twenty-five who professed conversion during the mission. Eighty-seven were under fifteen years of age, forty-three between fifteen and seventeen, and ninety-five over seventeen. The proportion of young people was much larger than usual in a colonial mission, and a most encouraging feature. Collections not only met expenditure, but left a substantial balance. The balance was divided among the other churches of the town, lest their funds should suffer because of the mission. Such action confirmed the good feeling among the churches, and was not without beneficial result among the unconverted. Since the mission, the minister writes: " We had a large attendance at the praise-meeting last Wednesday. A great many stood up and testified of God's converting grace. After a number had done so, I asked all present who had found Christ during the mission to stand up; and a great number rose to their feet. I then asked all who had received definite blessing of any kind to acknowledge it, and there stood up an exceeding great army. We added five names to the list of converts before the meeting closed." So the work went on, God was glorified, and His people filled with joy and praise.

After the mission the flame spread in a most wonderful manner. In the town and country places, for weeks afterwards, scarcely a service was held without conversions. Ministers and local preachers had the same experience; wherever they went they saw tears of penitence brightened into tears of joy, and confession of sin followed by hallelujahs of deliverance. A score of remarkable conversions have been reported to me; but I have space only to tell the story of one " Godlike miracle of love."

J. H. was a drunkard and blasphemer; "but prayer was made by the Church unto God for him." Not only was united supplication made on his behalf, but several persons interested themselves in his welfare. Foremost among these was a young man who had received the baptism of power at one of the afternoon meetings. J. H. had not attended a single meeting of the mission though asked often to do so. "One night," he afterwards said, "I went to the door of the hall; but the night was cold; so I thought it would be more comfortable at the 'pub'; so I spent the evening there." Two or three days after this, he had returned home after a day's debauch, and slept until far into the evening. "Going out to-night?" his wife asked. "No, I don't think I'll go out to-night." He took down the long neglected "Book" and began to read. The Holy Spirit shone on the page, and in his understanding; and there and then he realised his lost condition and felt himself "a condemned sinner." Conviction deepened. "Wife," said he at last, "I can stand this no longer. I'm going to kneel down and ask God to have mercy upon me; and you come and kneel down with me." She did as he requested. He prayed earnestly and long, and before they rose, "the dungeon flamed with light." Next morning he was in the minister's study, where, after telling "what great things the Lord had done for him," he signed the temperance pledge. Publicans look at the man and wonder. "Everyone in my house, even to little Tommy, knows I am changed; the hell has become a heaven." So he said a fortnight after his conversion.

For the measure of success vouchsafed to our efforts in New Zealand we give praise to God alone. Marvellous indeed were the results. During three months we conducted six missions, in connection with which over eighteen hundred persons were helped in the enquiry-rooms. But there are other results which cannot be presented in tabulated form. As a specimen, we quote the following paragraph from the *Advocate*, the local Methodist journal. The writer is a local correspondent in a most scattered district:—

"Peals of joy in heaven over good work here since the New Year. Our pastor went to attend one of the Rev. Thomas Cook's missions, and came back filled with faith, and a determination to look for definite results; and, of course, he got them. Over thirty have stood forth for Christ at our after-meetings, during the last two months, in different parts of the Circuit. Christian Endeavour Societies have been started at two centres. Never before has such spiritual progress been reported from this district."

The following testimony will avail to show the value and extent of the work. It is an extract from the pastoral address of the New Zealand Conference of 1895:—

"When it became known that the Rev. Thomas Cook would visit this colony for the purpose of conducting evangelistic services, a spirit of expectation was aroused throughout the whole Church. The knowledge of what God had wrought by the hand of His servant in other countries, and in the sister colonies, led us to look for a time of refreshing of a very special character. In this expectation we have not been disappointed. Abundant fruit has been gathered in every mission held. Hundreds of souls are rejoicing in a sense of sins forgiven as one result of Mr. Cook's labours, while hundreds more of God's people have been encouraged to enter into the promised land of perfect love."

It is but fair to mention that the earnest co-operation and practical sympathy of the ministers contributed largely towards these results. All were willing to sacrifice themselves to the interests of the work. The harmony and good feeling which existed between us and them was promoted largely by our sharing the hospitality of the manse. As I have already mentioned, our entertainment in the colonies was very frequently provided by the ministers. Living together, we came to a better understanding of each other than would have been possible otherwise. Our hearts were united, and, as a consequence, we speak more kindly and carefully, perhaps, of each other's work.

Of the future of New Zealand we have the largest hopes and expectations. The present commercial depression will soon be a thing of the past. It is the result, largely, of unwise borrowing of capital. These loans have demoralised the public generally, and have led to extravagance, discontent, and to taxes, which can be ill afforded. But the recuperative power of the colony is enormous. Favoured with a climate of unsurpassed salubrity, and with sources of wealth practically unlimited, it will soon overcome its difficulties, and immigrants will crowd to its shores. The Church is now doing foundation work. What is being done will mould and determine the future. The union of the Methodist bodies will add much to our influence as an aggressive and conservative force. By a decisive vote the Conference has decided to enter into an alliance with the United Methodist Free Church and the Bible Christian Church, they having signified their willingness to accept the Wesleyan basis of union. Undoubtedly, as a united Church, we shall be able to advance the interests of the Redeemer's Kingdom more effectually.

To be associated with the youth of a new nation is

no small privilege. We appreciated the responsibility the opportunity brought. If we have done anything towards helping to form the characters of those who will be the future rulers our purpose is accomplished.

"The ingenuity with which, during the last fifty years, the Church has attempted to construct new organisations for the recovery of men from sin and eternal death is unexampled; and now the question arises whether our machinery is not greater than our 'power.' A man with a large frame is often very weak because he has a small or feeble heart; and just now there seems reason to fear that the spiritual force of the Church is unequal to the enormous claims made upon it by the machinery it has to keep in motion. We are staggering under the weight of the tasks we have undertaken. Much of our work is very formal and mechanical. The channels in which our sympathies have to flow have become so numerous and so broad that the stream is almost stagnant. The extent and variety of our Christian work require that we should receive a fresh baptism of the Holy Ghost."— Dr. Dale.

CHAPTER X

NEW SOUTH WALES

Centenary Hall, Sydney—Armidale

WE had a pleasant passage from New Plymouth to Auckland, where we spent a few days before returning to Sydney. We made our home again with Mr. and Mrs. W. S. Wilson, whose unsparing hospitality, while we had the happiness of being their guests, it is one of our greatest pleasures to recall. A young man called on the Sunday afternoon to tell me that he had been converted in one of my English missions—at Walsall—in 1886. He is now a member of the Baptist Tabernacle, of which Thomas Spurgeon was, for some time, pastor. Mr. Shirley Baker, ex-premier of Tonga, also paid us a visit. I had written, some weeks before, to Rev. J. B. Watkin, who is now at the head of the Tongan Free Church, offering to conduct a series of missions in the Friendly Islands, if the Wesleyan and Free Churches would work together. My one idea was to promote a better feeling between the Churches, as I had heard of the rivalry which existed, and of the harm it was doing. So I proposed that I should preach alternately for the two Churches, and that both parties should attend all the services, and help each other. Mr. Watkin replied as follows:

—" I am afraid that there are too many difficulties in the way of your proposed visit to the Friendly Islands on an evangelistic tour. I feel that the situation is too much strained for a united invitation to be sent to you. Thanking you very sincerely for your wish to visit us, and trusting that your labour in the colonies may continue to be successful." Our own minister in Tonga welcomed the proposal most heartily, but as the Churches would not unite in the invitation, we did not go. Mr. Baker explained, as the reason why the Free Church would not unite in the invitation, that it was feared we had other aims than those purely spiritual. We had a long conversation concerning the disastrous strife which had led to the division, from which I gathered that if Mr. Baker could live those years over again, he would act differently.

Dr. Talmage speaks of the "stormy stream" between New Zealand and Australia; but on our return journey it was unusually peaceful. In less than four days we arrived at Sydney, where we were heartily welcomed by the Rev. Rainsford Bavin. Mr. Bavin is a native of Lincolnshire. He comes of a grand old Methodist stock, and inherits the blessing that is always the heritage of those whose forefathers have been men of God. At twelve years of age he was soundly converted, and at sixteen he became a local preacher. After a course of study under the direction of the Rev Dr. Kesson, Mr. Bavin sailed for New Zealand in 1867 to do missionary work. His energy of character and pulpit and platform ability, together with his loving disposition, soon secured for him the affection and respect of the people, and of his brethren. In 1883 he was elected to the chair of

VIEW OF SYDNEY.

the Conference, being one of the youngest men ever raised to that dignity. The trend of his ministry may be inferred from the motto he selected for the year of his presidency : " A revival in every Circuit in the Connexion." After serving his Church in Circuit work, both in New Zealand and New South Wales, with unusual acceptance and success, he was appointed to take charge of the work at the Centenary Hall, Sydney, when the Rev. W. G. Taylor visited England a few years ago. Not only was Mr. Bavin able to sustain the work so auspiciously begun by Mr. Taylor, but, during his superintendency, marked progress was made in every direction. It was during his appointment to the Hall, that we held our mission there.

We found every kind of agency, such as the London mission employs, in active operation. Congregations were overflowing, and never a Sabbath passed, in the ordinary services, but several declared their determination to live a new life. Because of constant conversions reported at the hall, we had some fears, at first, lest our visit would not yield the same return as at a place where conversions were not so frequent. Our fears, however, were soon dispelled. Centrally situated, in the midst of a teeming population, new material is always within easy access. The five mission bands brought in crowds of new faces to each service; and from the suburbs Christians came with their unconverted friends, until the hall was far too small to accommodate those who wished to hear. Special counsel was given to workers on the first Saturday night with regard to the best means of helping those to Christ who were seeking Him. " What to do and what *not* to do," was the subject;

and it certainly bore good fruit in the enquiry-rooms afterwards.

Midday meetings for business men and others were wonderfully blessed. My addresses at these dealt broadly with sanctification, each discourse treating of some distinct phase of the doctrine. The interest grew to such an extent, that many came with lunch, sewing, or reading, quite an hour before service time. Ministers from many churches were present in large number. Waves of such holy feeling occasionally swept over us that tears of joy flowed down many a cheek, and scores were raised to a higher platform of Christian experience. If the human face is a thermometer of the heart's feeling, moments of rapture were felt by many. The local Methodist paper says: "Ideals of holiness seemed to be lifted to a higher plane. The vast audience listened breathlessly lest a word should be lost. There was no mawkish sentiment, but wholesome teaching, for which numbers bless God. The best fruitage of these holiness talks will be their translation into life's commoner business." An average attendance of a thousand persons each noon indicated the hunger which exists for spiritual food, and a healthy, powerful vitality, for which we could not but feel profoundly thankful.

The evening services were all seasons of power and refreshing. The eager look of the sea of faces, and the hush pervading, proved the presence and power of God, and the earnestness of human hearts. Interest deepened, and numbers increased as the mission proceeded. Converts multiplied. A large percentage were men. Indeed, it was particularly noted that men were in the majority at all the meetings. This is refreshing in the face of a recent long press correspondence in the colonies on the question, "Why do not men go to church?"

In order to present definite issues, and gain specific results, three special services were organised. On the Friday night we had a young people's rally. The flower of Methodist homes and Sunday schools gathered *en masse*. Belief that many conversions would follow that service was not disappointed. Ninety-two decided for Christ, all above twelve years of age. The majority were senior scholars from suburban schools. On Sunday afternoon the service for "men only" was held. Our accommodation was taxed to the uttermost. The sight was unusually inspiring, and the singing defies description. As I explained that as we sin we may expect to be sinned against; that while God forgives the past it still remains as a fact; and as I expounded the laws of heredity, many were visibly affected. The hush of the Divine presence was in the throng. Aged, middle-life, and stalwart young men sought mercy and pardon in tears. That afternoon thirty-five professed conversion. The third special service was on the Tuesday afternoon, for "women only." Whether or not there is more religious instinct in women than in men is debatable; but certainly in Sydney they outdid the men. Long before the time fixed for the opening of the meeting hundreds crowded the hall entrances, and although two thousand secured sitting or standing room, hundreds had to be barred out. This phenomenal service was consummated by large accessions to the cause of Christ.

Whole families turned to God. The baser sort as well as respectable were cleansed. Presbyterians, Baptists, Lutherans, Roman Catholics, and Quakers were among those who professed conversion. The registered number of converts was four hundred and four; but many trusted Christ who did not enter the enquiry-rooms. The majority of the enquirers were over twenty-five years of age. Among them was a Chinaman, a prize-fighter, a publican's wife, an ex-city missionary, a policeman, and the organist of one of the Anglican churches.

Faith in God, and united, concentrated Christian effort were abundantly strengthened and confirmed. Requests for prayer poured in, and were laid before Him, who created prayer instincts. One night one hundred and three requests were read, having reference to three hundred different persons. Some of the answers received read like a chapter of Wesley's journal. An influence mysterious, subtle, penetrating, pervaded the services. To those who understand these things it was unmistakably Divine power. These influences, with the unbounded enthusiasm and far-reaching results, mark the mission as truly heaven-born as any we have conducted. To ministers and people alike it came as a stimulant and encouragement. That it should summarily end at the height of its glory was regrettable; but the results will remain. The time test is the best test. It was so in the beautiful Parable of the Sower. Transient emotion and enthusiasm die away. It is as a man's convictions that his life is. We have endeavoured to produce such convictions as will remain in the rough-and-tumble of the world's life, and God has graciously worked with us "confirming the Word." All honour be to His name. All real success results from the unction of the Holy One resting on and filling the messenger and accompanying the message. In no other power can spiritual victories be won. "It is the Lord's doing, and it is marvellous in our eyes."

Workers in the enquiry-rooms furnished details which cannot all be given. These are examples:—

After the young people's service, a minister said, "Four of our young folks have decided to-night. Here they are—one, two, three." "Who is the fourth?" he asked one of his teachers. "Your wife's sister," was the reply, when his eyes filled with tears as he murmured his praises to the God that answereth prayer. "Three servants from the same home have been all seeking together," announced another worker. "A father and mother are there rejoicing over their son," said a third, pointing to a happy group in a corner of the building. "He is sixteen years of age, and they have hoped for this for years." "Two from the choir to-night," said the lay missionary as he praised God aloud, and pleaded with another to decide. These are some of the greetings I received when I came from the pulpit after I had closed the service. A Scandinavian told me, in broken English, how his heart had been melted by the singing. He had come from Charters Towers on business, intending to return immediately, but remained to the end of the mission. A man-of-war's man sent for me from the enquiry-room on the first Sunday night. He had just found peace with God, and said he wished to tell me what had led to his conversion. For some weeks he had been training for a prize-fight, having heard that some colonial had offered to fight any Englishman who would represent the "old country"; he, the colonial, would represent the colonies. Obtaining a few days leave from his ship, the man-of-war's man had stood in the ring on the Saturday night accepting the challenge, but his opponent did not appear. On the Sunday morning he was met in the street by an artilleryman, who asked him where he was going. "Nowhere particular," was his reply; so his friend urged him to come to the hall and hear the English evangelist. He consented when he heard the name of the preacher, "because," he said, "I believe he is the same man who was at Portsmouth some years ago when a brother of mine was converted." The word at the morning service touched his heart so powerfully, that he resolved to attend in the evening. He had been a Christian fifteen years before, and, said he, "If there has been a more miserable man on God's earth than others, I have been the man since I lost the sense of the Divine favour." Chords which had been broken vibrated again that night, and he was among the first to enter the enquiry-room. "Now it is all right again," he testified; "God has forgiven me, and I mean to serve Him. I shall go back to the ship and they shall all know on which side I am. But it is strange how I got to this hall to-day," he added. "God only knows how my heart has ached to have back again what I lost when I left the Lord." In such "miracles of grace" the Holy Spirit manifests His being and power. What weak men fail to do in years, He does quickly. By making effective the most unlikely means and instrumentalities the Spirit is honoured, and the supernatural character of the work is established. There were many other such cases of rare interest.

Not a single service was held without a collection. When I protested against this, I was told it was the custom, and the people were pleased to help. And so it proved. Looking into the collection plates on the second Sunday, I asked where the coppers were, and was astonished to learn that, until recently, coppers were never given in Australia at collections. All gave silver or gold. Now that the people are poorer, coppers are beginning to appear, but not to any considerable extent. My curiosity led me to ask for particulars concerning one day's collections, the result was as follows:—

	£	s.	d.
83 pennies	0	6	11
1304 threepennies	16	6	0
415 sixpences	10	7	6
82 shillings	4	2	0
7 florins	0	14	0
3 half-crowns	0	7	6
1 half-sovereign	0	10	0
	£32	13	11

Let it be remembered that those who attend the hall are chiefly of the working-class, and the poor who do not care to attend respectable churches, and it will be evident that the Australians give, proportionately, much more than those who attend our English churches. Our missions not only were rich in blessings spiritual, but, in almost every place we visited, a substantial credit balance remained for the benefit of the Circuit after all expenses were paid. The result and order are, souls converted first, then pockets. If ministers would always put "first things first," there would be no difficulty about financial matters.

Mention has already been made of the midday meetings, at which I gave a series of addresses bearing more particularly upon the cultivation of the higher Christian life. These were attended not only by our own people, but by members of other churches, especially Episcopalians, who had been influenced by the teaching of the Keswick Conventions. It is remarkable how far-reaching the influence of that Convention has been. Wherever we went we met some who owed impetus and spiritual elevation to the teaching that had been given there. Of the visit to Australia of the Rev. G. C. Grubb, one of the Keswick speakers, scores whom we personally met spoke most gratefully. Many who were converted under his ministry, and others who received the Pentecostal baptism, told us their story; and we saw with our own eyes the power of Divine grace in their lives. The mere verbal and definitional differences, which divide the Keswick and Wesleyan teachers of holiness in England, are not allowed to separate those in Australia who believe " He is able to save to the uttermost." Both parties agree so enthusiastically on so much concerning this glorious life of faith as a distinct experience, that they agree to differ in their terminology, in the phrases they use to express what is practically the same thing. Instead of contending whether a principle of evil still remains in the nature after the heart is cleansed from all sin, or whether, as we Wesleyans put it, the Almighty Saviour conditionally expels from the entire nature the very inbeing of sin, and that the infirmities incident to earthly limitations are covered by the Atonement, which is always needed, they avoid much of this doctrinal hair-splitting, and with a unity of purpose, such as we might well copy, give themselves to the far more sensible and Christly endeavour to arouse believers to claim all their heritage in Christ Jesus, to take Him to be a complete Saviour. The experience is the same by whatever terms it may be described. It is this brotherly blending of the different schools of thought in Australia that explains, largely, the interest aroused on the subject, and the headway the holiness movement is making in all the churches. Among our ministers, and those of other Methodist churches, an association has been formed "to unite together those members of the various branches of the Methodist Church who have obtained the blessing of entire sanctification, for the purpose of strengthening each other's hands in God, and for associated effort, in various directions, for the purpose of making known throughout the land this great doctrine of Holy Writ." Great blessing has resulted from the Conventions held under the auspices of the association; and the paper they publish, *Glad Tidings*, is, increasingly, a source of good. There is no more hopeful feature in the work of God in New South Wales than the attention that is being given to the higher Christian experiences, and the possibilities of faith.

How the influence of the work in Sydney was felt even by those labouring among the heathen in the South Sea Islands, the following letter, published by Dr. George Brown in the *Missionary Review*, will reveal. It was written by the Rev. William Brown, one of our missionaries in New Britain:—

"We have read with great interest the various reports of the Rev. Thomas Cook's mission services in the colonies; and as we read the letter of a dear sister describing the work of God in Stanmore Circuit, we wished that we could only take a flying trip and join in such a work. We were greatly profited, also, by reading the life of the evangelist, and also the account of his tour in South Africa. We were especially interested in reading of his preaching and conducting mission services in South Africa through an interpreter.

"All these things impressed us greatly; and we sought, by close thinking and earnest prayer, to see how we, too, could share in the wave of blessing. We felt a little afraid, at first, of starting a week's special services among these people. However, the Rev. W. J. Chambers, of New Britain (who also had enjoyed the reading of Rev. Thomas Cook's life), settled our wavering resolutions on the matter by commencing a week of special effort at the village of Nodup; and the results were grand. All glory to God!

"Then our brother, and his faithful native teachers, held a week of services at Matupit, and God greatly blessed them there. I do not know the numerical results, but hope that Mr. Chambers will write you a full account for the *Review*. The work of God in New Britain has received a new impulse, and we are looking and believing for good times.

"Being forcibly impressed with the necessity of putting forth every effort to strengthen the spiritual life of our new members, to reclaim the fallen ones and to save sinners, we have decided to hold one week's special services each month, and to visit, in turn, each town that has had a teacher resident in it for a number of years; for we feel sure that it would be useless to go to a town where the people do not, as yet, understand the rudiments of the gospel.

"Last week we determined to commence operations at Urukuk, a little town not far from our mission-house. We commenced on the Sunday evening, and held a service each night, and finished on Saturday. During all the meetings we felt the presence of God to be very near to us, and, what was best of all, precious souls were saved. During the seven services there were twenty-three seekers, of whom some were members seeking for more spiritual life, and some were backsliders seeking again for the peace which they had lost through inconsistency of conduct. Since the meetings closed, a man and his wife have been to the teacher, earnestly desiring to live better lives, and asking to be admitted among God's people. Truly, 'God's arm is not shortened that it cannot save.'

"Rejoice with us, all ye friends of missions, and help us, by your prayers, to look forward to greater blessing."

From the letter written by the Rev. W. J. Chambers, to which reference is made by Mr. Brown, we extract the following:—

"The work is still going on, and many are deciding for Christ. I do wish you were here just now to help with your advice. There are so many questions I would like to ask you which I care not to write.

I feel this revival work is awfully responsible work, yet I dare not shrink from it. Every care is taken to instruct each enquirer in the way of salvation; and I personally investigate each case, and endeavour to deal faithfully with them as one who must give an account to God.

"Still I, at times, feel, with the hard work of these meetings, together with the great responsibility, quite worn out. I trust you will not think me fainthearted. No! I am devoutly thankful to God for these evidences of His favour. But there are times when I would be so glad to be able to seek advice and help from one who has had experience in mission work, and upon whose decision I could rely confidently. We have held two weeks' special services in parts of Raluana section, with the result that about seventy-five have professed conversion.

"To-night we began a week's mission at Raluana. Fully five hundred people came together for the service, and we had fifty inquirers after salvation. . . . I feel that now is our time to put forth every effort to strengthen our position in this land. I fully believe I have the confidence of every chief, and, I might say, the large majority of the people, throughout my territory; and never before was there such an opportunity for doing good work."

What the religious press thought about the work will interest those who are concerned to know the best methods of soul-winning. Evangelism is a science, and needs to be studied as such. Souls are to be won, and he who wins them is wise. While realising emphatically that the work is God's work, and that all our efforts are vain without Him, we have a part to perform, and even God will not do our work without us, without our skill and adaptation. For years the Church has been praying God to save the nations, and all the time He has been looking to us to do it. We are to "Go, and disciple the nations."

The fact is God seldom works apart from human instrumentalities.

> "Not God Himself can make man's best,
> Without best men to help Him."

This is not heresy or irreverence. If we fail to do our part there will be defeat, and perhaps failure. Hence the art of soul-saving must be cultivated. To win souls there is required, in addition to personal consecration, tact, adaptation of means to the end, knowledge of human nature, and much else which comes only as the result of close and careful observation. It is true that God alone can save men; but there is a sense in which we can do it. There is something that requires wisdom, something which, if we do it wisely, will insure the conversion of sinners in proportion to the wisdom employed. "He that winneth souls is wise." The following article was written by the Editor of *The Methodist*, the official organ of the New South Wales Conference. Its observations bear upon the point:—

"THE NEW REVIVALISM

" We hear of the ' The New Theology ' and ' The New Pulpit': it is only in keeping that we should, also, have what may be called ' The New Revivalism.' Not but it may be, after all, a very old revivalism, and, therefore, new, like some of the old Methodist tunes, so antique as to be perfectly novel to the present generation. The Rev. Thomas Cook may be taken as a type of the new revivalist, and as exhibiting the latest methods in evangelistic work. Evangelistic services have become associated, in the minds of a good many, with depreciatory characteristics; with twaddle and gush, and maudlin sentiment, and rant, and appeals to fear; with tautological vapidness and stale anecdotes. How far this estimate is just, we do not pretend to say; but it exists and widely so. It is, therefore, in the interests of the truth itself, and for the benefit of the community at large, that the message of the Redeemer should be proclaimed, in professedly revival meetings, in such a way that the respect of men should be gained for it, and the robust minds of practical artisans and shrewd business men be attracted with sympathy. Every earnest preacher has his own way, and the noisy, demonstrative, or emotional style is natural to some, and also attractive to some hearers, and may be quite right in both cases; but the evil comes in when it becomes generally accepted that there is no earnest preaching or evangelistic effort without these peculiarities. Mr. Cook's fame and success are not due to following the usual grooves, nor to adopting already stereotyped ways of procedure. He is not noisy, but quiet and self-restrained; not wordy, but terse, his sentences being pruned and phrases compressed, or crisp and sharp. He does not talk childishly, which mode some soul-seekers adopt as the surest way to catch men, but speaks strong common sense, such as men like to listen to; nor is his subject matter gospel-and-water, with the aqueous preponderating, but well-reasoned, fresh, logical, suggestive, and impressive thought. His addresses, too, are carefully constructed and cumulative in their effect; they are well designed instruments rather than products. And they are certainly not lacking in heat and glow. There is fire, intense, moral earnestness, not the consecrating flame leaping from crackling thorns, but the rose warmth that appears in the red-hot bar of iron. It may now be possible for quiet men who have a way of their own, and to whom restrained, more than manifested, emotion is the more natural to feel, that even they may aim at souls with a prospect of saving some. And congregations may be encouraged to recognise in men who are not of the Boanerges, nor of the Jeremiah, class, true evangelists for their Lord, from whom may even be expected gracious results in time. Thomas Cook's mission will, in this way, be a stimulant and encouragement to ministers and people.

"There is another feature about this 'New Revivalism' which is specially interesting, and that is its suggestion of the apostolic method. We cannot see that the apostles, in order to fix conviction in sinners' consciences, and to gain adherents to the new Church, ever played the harlequin, or made sacred things absurd, or that they adopted what was *outré* and fantastic that they 'might by all means save some.' Their mode appears to have been manly, straight, dignified (by which is meant natural, not official dignity), yet easy, and consumingly in earnest. They gained respect as well as notoriety, and their message was as weighty and serious as it was novel. Greek art has been defined as 'the perfection of common sense.' In that sense there was the highest art about the apostolic words and methods. It was radiant, too, with the sunny smiles of hope and joy. Christianity, as they administered it, brought a great cheerfulness into the world. And while there was no trace of the convulsive, or contortive, or maudlin, there was unmistakable, *power*. An influence, mysterious, subtle, penetrating, soul-compelling, pervaded their work. And it was in that the Apostle Paul so openly delighted; he who could have plumed himself on scholarship, social culture, dialectic power, and profound knowledge of Rabbinical lore, with an academic acquaintance with Greek philosophy, esteemed these things lightly (though using them with considerable effect), but rejoiced in a power, distinct from them all, that he knew he possessed, and which was the secret of his success with men. Now Mr. Cook has a remarkable harvest wherever he sows a mission; but it is difficult to connect cause with effect, or rather, to account for so much effect from the causes under observation, unless on the assumption that St. Paul made with regard to his own work. And so, as we study the 'New Revivalism,' as it is going on at the Centenary Hall just now, the words come forcibly to our minds: 'And my speech and my preaching was not with enticing words of man's wisdom, but in demonstration of the Spirit and of power; that your faith should not stand in the wisdom of men, but in the power of God.' 'Through mighty signs and wonders, by the power of the Spirit of God, so that from Jerusalem and round about unto Illyricum I have fully preached the gospel of

MR. JOHN CORBETT.

Christ. 'For our gospel came not unto you in word only, but also in power, and in the Holy Ghost, and in much assurance.' The words become quite realistic as we watch Thomas Cook's mission."

It was remarked in Sydney, as a curious coincidence, that while I, a Middlesboro' man, was there doing missionary work, another Middlesboro' man, the Rev. W. G. Taylor, should have gone from Sydney to plead for, and to do, mission work in England. We met, at the Centenary Hall, Mr. Edward Hutchinson, another fellow-townsman, whom we had known as an earnest worker before he left the old country. He is now one of the lay missionaries of the Hall staff, doing splendid service for the Master, and greatly beloved by all the people. Mention of Sydney always brings to mind one other genial face. I refer to the affable, sharp, and clear-headed manager of the Wesleyan Book Depôt, Mr. John Corbett. His patience, consideration, and unfailing courtesy and kindness make him live in our affection, as he does in that of all who know him, because he is everybody's friend. The success of the depôt, under his care, is, in a large measure, the result of his business qualities, and his cordial relations with the whole of the Australian Methodist world.

Ten days at Armidale, a small town on the main line between Sydney and Brisbane, brought to a conclusion our work in New South Wales. The town is situated four thousand feet above the level of the sea, and is a great resort for invalids during the hot weather. The district around has been named New England, because the climate somewhat resembles that of our country. Our church not being large enough for the mission, the Town Hall was engaged, the spacious stage undergoing a remarkable transformation for enquiry-room purposes, for which it answered admirably. Though not numerically strong, our people were full of energetic faith. With a membership of not more than fifty, they had supported a minister for years; and in preparing for our visit they manifested the same self-reliance and confidence. The spirit of consecration and faith rose high, and right royally did our risen Lord answer His people's prayers. Hearers came from all the district around; some drove more than a hundred miles to share in the feast. Such religious gatherings had never been known in the town before. On the first Sabbath the hall was crowded, and, before the mission closed, the building proved to be far too small. No service was held without conversions. These so increased, during the ten days, that more than three hundred names were taken of those who had professed decision for Christ. Among the seekers were many relatives of our workers, "just the sort we were most anxious to win for Christ," one of them said. "My father was the man who led Peter M'Kenzie to the Saviour," said a fine stalwart fellow, after he had told us how he had left home as a youth, wild and wayward; but he could never get away, he said, from the influences of the home in which he had been reared. Another of the converts was a fruiterer, who had been accustomed to sell on the Sabbath day. The day following his conversion a paper was pasted in front of his shop, announcing that nothing, in future, would be sold there on the Sabbath. Several railway men were among the converts. One had had a quarrel with another, who, strange to say, had decided to serve God the same night. They shook hands in the enquiry-room, and as they did so, one remarked, "Now I have decided to be a Christian, I must be reconciled to man as well as to God." These are representative cases. The whole Circuit shared in the blessing. "The mission will work an era in the history of Methodism here," wrote a correspondent. Best of all, the work did not end with the mission. Each Sabbath after we left conversions were reported at all the chief centres. A revival broke out at Uralla soon afterwards, in which, during one week, forty conversions were secured. The whole district was glad with the presence, and vocal with the praises of Jesus. Blessed work this, to bring men, through Christ, into fellowship with the Heavenly Father, who yearns with unutterable love over our fallen race.

George Herbert's words are true—

> "All earthly joys grow less
> In the one joy of doing kindliness."

WESLEYAN CHURCH, BRISBANE.

CHAPTER XI

QUEENSLAND

Brisbane—Ipswich—Rockhampton—Townsville—Charters Towers

ON our way from Armidale to Brisbane we spent a day at Tenterfield, where I preached, afternoon and evening, to large and attentive congregations. After the evening sermon, I asked those to remain who wished to have the plan of salvation explained to them, and to my astonishment all the congregation remained. The half-hour which followed was most impressive, and will long be remembered by many. We arrived at Brisbane on Friday, May 31st, and found several ministers and friends waiting at the station to receive us. Among these was the Hon. F. T. Brentnall, whose hospitality we shared. Mr. Brentnall is nephew of Mr. Thomas Brentnall, of Middlesboro', who was my mother's class leader, and superintendent of the Sunday school which I attended when a lad. These connections soon caused us to feel at home with each other, and helped much to make our visit the pleasure it was.

Our mission was held in the Albert Street Church, one of the most beautiful church buildings in Queensland. It is built of red brick, with dressings of stone. A spire towers to the height of one hundred and twenty-five feet above the pavement, forming a commanding object, which is visible from most parts of the city. A leading feature of the design, which is of Gothic order, is the enclosed cloisters which surround the building, and serve the same purpose as the wide verandahs on private dwelling-houses—that of keeping the interior cool. The pulpit is of polished cedar, almost severely simple in design, while the other furniture is of polished pine. A beautiful gasalier of brass, which hangs from the centre of the ceiling, is a conspicuous object, as is also the grand organ, which is behind the pulpit, facing the congregation. Until recently this organ was the finest instrument in Queensland, and even yet holds a premier place in public opinion, as is proved by the crowded audiences at the weekly Saturday night recitals, conducted by the organist, Mr. Benson, R.A.M.

On the Saturday night when we commenced our work, the President of the Conference introduced us, and promised, on behalf of the seven Circuits interested in the mission, a loving and hearty co-operation. Between three and four hundred workers were present, to whom I explained our methods of work, and how to promote a revival spirit. We knew the battle was already won before we parted, and joined in singing the doxology for what was about to be seen, heard, and felt.

The time for holding the mission could not have been better. The weather was perfect, cool, and bright, with a good moon. No competing attractions interfered. From the first the church was filled with an eager congregation; but, towards the end, the enormous crowds which assembled, not only densely packed the church, but hundreds went away unable to find standing room. Additional chairs were placed wherever possible, but half an hour at least before service time the place was filled. The churchyard accommodation for horses and vehicles was taxed to the utmost by suburban and country people, who came in all sorts of conveyances, from aristocratic waggonettes to hawkers' spring-carts. As many as fifty vehicles might be counted at a single service. Even at the service for men only, scores had to be turned away. It was a memorable and inspiring sight to look into the dense sea of faces of men of all ages, as they listened "rapt and eager" to our message. It seemed as if they were hungering for the good old "bread of life." There was no modernised theory of religion, no phases of the so-called new gospel in our discourses. We pursued the old lines, emphasised and enforced the old truths, proclaimed the old salvation, and it was this the men came to hear. The "old, old story" will save the world yet. Conversions rejoiced our hearts at every service. The young came, the middle-aged, and here and there the greyhaired; all sorts and conditions were wounded by the Spirit's sword. Ministers and friends led these to the Saviour, and saw mourning turned to joy. Besides those who sought the Lord openly, others rejoiced over experiences made more deep and definite by fresh appropriations of the divine provisions. No statistics can represent the results. Spiritual facts such as these defy tabulation. Nothing was more wonderful than the drawing together of God's people to one another and to Him.

"Brisbane Methodism," says a local paper, "has felt the breath of spring, the desert is rejoicing and blossoming as the rose, the time for the singing of birds has come. Not for many a day, if ever before, have such times been experienced in Queensland. If this gracious and glorious beginning is followed up, and we believe it will, through the colony, a red-letter epoch has been made in our history. A 'heavenly vision' has brought our true aim and goal more distinctly into view, and the determination has been renewed to pursue it with greater singleness of eye, with more hopeful courage, and simpler and stronger faith in God."

Turning to actual accessions, the names of four hundred and sixty-nine persons were taken in the enquiry-rooms:— Wesleyans, 252; Baptists, 54; Presbyterians, 35; Anglicans, 30; Primitive Methodists, 25; Congregationalists, 16; Salvation Army, 3; Lutherans, 3; not mentioned, 37; no church, 9; undecided, 3. It was a fine sight to look around, at the converts' meeting, on so many young men and women, but with many of mature age scattered among them, saying, by their presence in seats specially reserved, that they were definitely committed to the service of the Lord. Deepest feeling prevailed as glad testimonies were freely given by those who had found the Saviour. Ministers and people praised God together for the harvest gathered from fields in which they had sown with tearful eyes. Several hymns were sung between the testimonies, and, from first to last, a deep enthusiasm was manifested. The service closed with the following resolution, proposed by Rev. W. A. Harrison, and seconded by the President of the Conference:—"That this meeting, filling the Albert Street Church, consisting of over four hundred persons who have given themselves to God during the mission, and over four hundred others, declares its deepest thanks to Almighty God for answering the prayers of the Church by pouring out His Spirit over Brisbane and the surrounding neighbourhood. It also expresses its thanks to the Rev. Thomas Cook for his faithful ministry, during which he spoke the words that reached our hearts, calling us to repentance and consecration." The resolution was carried by the whole audience rising to their feet and singing heartily the doxology. Hundreds are saying, "He hath put a new song into my mouth." "It was worth all the mission," a minister writes, "for the help I have received." Another says: "We shall speak in renewed tones of confidence, courage, and command now." A third testifies: "We shall be encouraged to adhere more closely to the old lines of doctrine and the old methods of salvation, and to pursue our work with stronger hope of success." The general joy and gladness which prevailed was evidenced by the congregation standing each night, after the service closed, on the elevated terrace in front of the church, and singing, lustily, hymns of praise. This filled the radiating streets with music, and caused many to exclaim, "We have seen strange things to-day." The full results of such a mission can be known only in eternity.

No better illustration could be given of the interest awakened by the mission than the following paragraph, which I have clipped from a local religious paper:—

"Mr. Cook's work in the Albert Street Church, as a central mission for the city of Brisbane and its suburbs, has been an undoubted success. A friend who went to the door of the church on the Sunday afternoon, when there was a service for men only, tried every door to get in, but could not manage it. 'It was a regular jam,' he says, 'and the finest sight of the kind I have seen.' Some few of the knowing used to say that not more than eight hundred people could be got into the building, but sixteen hundred tickets were taken on this occasion, and some got in without tickets. Our friend got in at last to the organ loft, and climbed the ladder of the towering instrument in order to see the throng, which, he said, was magnificent. The atmosphere, also, was reported upon as being very thick. A good many people stood in the corridors, but Mr. Cook spoke out so well that they could hear almost all he said.

"People were variously affected by his discourses, and some very decent folk not at all. Still one could not help seeing the power he exerted. As far as I could judge, those who were influenced by him were those who are in the habit of attending church, the kind of people who think, and not the 'weekly washers.' The evening service was to have commenced at 7.30; but as the church was packed as tight as it could hold by 7, it began at 7.5. A helper, who had been packing the people like herring in the gallery, worked his way out to get a little fresh air for himself, and then could not get back again, and, as even every window was occupied, went with some others to Mr. Buchanan's Presbyterian Church, which received no small augmentation from the overflow."

A large and carefully-trained choir rendered valuable service, and added considerably to the interest of the meetings. Australians seem to be more musical than the average Englishman. While there may not be among them so much of the scholarly appreciation of the classical musical standards, as exists in England, there does seem to be a more general taste for music, as was evidenced by the choirs got together for our missions. Often these were more than a hundred strong, and their singing of the special hymns we asked for, was a great attraction and blessing.

The following letter illustrates the profound feelings of gratitude to God felt by His people for the prayers He answered and the blessing He gave:—

"I cannot refrain from writing with reference to your late mission in Brisbane. That God has blessed and honoured you in the mission on which He has sent you, hundreds bear witness, and we rejoice still more in the power of the blessed gospel. As a member of the committee appointed to make arrangements for your visit, I thank and bless God for your coming. As a Sunday-school teacher, I praise His name for the conversion of one of my class, and the building up of the others. As a brother, I give thanks to Him for blessing a sister-in-law; and, as a husband, I rejoice with a joy unspeakable, that my wife was led to give herself to God on the last night of your mission. And still more, as a Christian, I praise Him for blessings to my own soul. 'What shall I render unto the Lord for all His benefits?' I am constrained to ask. 'I will take the cup of salvation and call upon the name of the Lord.' . . ."

Such testimonies might be multiplied. " Songs of rejoicing and gladness " did indeed fill the hearts of the people. The ransomed of the Lord did return, and come to Zion with songs and everlasting joy upon their heads. We closed the mission praising and blessing God.

Ten days were all too short for Brisbane, with its population of nearly a hundred thousand persons; but arrangements had been made with Ipswich, which, like the laws of the Medes and Persians, could not be altered, so we were obliged to leave when the work was fullest of power and promise. Ipswich has a population of ten thousand, and is distant from Brisbane twenty-four miles by rail. It is an old-fashioned town, with a reputation for sobriety and religion much in advance of most colonial towns. In no town of the same size have we found a more vigorous Methodism. In attachment to our doctrines and policy, and for solidity and spiritual fervour, the Church is much more English-like than colonial. A more united and lovingly zealous people we never worked among.

Having learned that in Australia, the same as in England, there are many whom Mr. Gladstone would designate " Oncers,"—those who attend Divine worship once on the Sabbath day, and are then content with having satisfied the demands of Christian duty,—I made it a custom, in the later missions I held, to preach in the morning service the sort of sermon I had generally reserved for the evening. By this means some were awakened who would not have been with us in the evening, and among these were some of our best converts. Ministers who make it an invariable rule to preach to Christians in the morning and to the unconverted at night, might occasionally reverse their mode of procedure with the best results. At Ipswich the first Sunday morning service was one of the most solemn and impressive of the whole series. Many who were afterwards converted spoke of that service as the time when they were awakened to a sense of their need. Nearly a hundred of all ages sought counsel in the enquiry-rooms the first Sabbath. As the week advanced the meetings were increasingly full of unction and power. Christians came in hundreds, from far and near, to hear the glad evangel of a full salvation. The closing service exceeded all others in numbers and seekers. All the available space was occupied, seats, pews, aisles, and doorways. The superintendent minister managed to secure a seat on one of the steps that led to the choir platform, while his colleagues shared the organ seat. The preacher had about two square feet to stand upon. That night will not soon be forgotten in Ipswich. How mightily the power of God was present to save! How fascinated and spellbound the people seemed to be! Who could witness those hundreds of pairs of eyes fixed with such intensity on the preacher, and say that the old soul-saving doctrines have lost their power! It was a day of God's right hand. Before it closed, one hundred, save one, professed conversion. Was it any wonder that the people wept for joy, and with a loud voice praised the Lord? Taking the whole mission, three hundred and thirty made public confession of having decided for Christ; but this by no means represents all that God wrought. Wonderful uplifts came to some, clearer views of the life of faith to others, while to all the sufficiency, power, and attractiveness of the old gospel were made manifest, as seldom if ever before.

Referring to the praise and testimony meeting held after the mission, the minister wrote: "When I threw the meeting open for testimony, I had scarcely got seated before a young lady was on her feet telling of God's goodness to her, and then for nearly an hour testimonies were given, with snatches of praise between, until seventy had spoken. One man said he had been a backslider for years, and came to one of the meetings through curiosity, but when he got into the church and saw the crowd the thought came to him, 'How much greater will the crowd be on the Judgment Day.' That led him to think and to return to Christ."

"Nearly a dozen of our hands have been converted," wrote an employer of labour, "and still the work goes on." "Eight others decided for Christ at the praise-meeting," says another, "and we are continually hearing of those who were led to Christ in the mission who did not enter the enquiry-rooms." Within a month of the mission we heard of four deaths among those who had attended the meetings. Two were converts, only just in time; but it was all right, their friends are comforted by the remembrance of their triumph in death. Mr. Joseph Foote, with whom we stayed, wrote: "We are not the only Christians who got a great blessing. Many others have been helped to claim a full salvation." Our memories of Ipswich and of the friends we met there, are all pleasant.

Our last three missions were held at Rockhampton, Charters Towers, and Townsville — in central and northern Queensland. The appalling religious indifference which prevails there was a new experience.

Not more than twenty per cent. of the population ever attend a place of worship. Sports and secular concerts are often held on the Sabbath. Religion is scouted, by the great majority, as only fit for a puritanical age. We found small memberships in the churches, but little prestige or social status, and much discouragement among ministers and godly folk. For the first few days our hearers and converts were nearly all women. Do what we would, we could not secure the presence of the sterner sex until the meeting for men only, which, in each town, not only brought an accession of power, but seemed to turn the tide in our favour. Afterwards the men came, not only to the meetings, but to the Saviour, and a new religious instinct was, for the time, created. By those who know Queensland and the other colonies best, the seven hundred seekers over whom we rejoiced in these three towns, was considered a more remarkable work of God than anything we had previously reported. The figures by no means represent the extent of blessing vouchsafed; and we left the churches full of new life and hope.

From Rockhampton the superintendent wrote: "Last Monday we had our social gathering, and although it was confined to converts, workers, and the choir, our church was crammed. It was a splendid meeting, full of inspiration and hope for the future. The seven o'clock prayer-meeting on Sunday morning was attended by sixty or seventy people, and we intend to keep it going. Another proof of the truth of your remark, that sometimes missions are 'a last call,' has been furnished. One of the converts at the men's meeting was drowned the day after you left. A good woman who got converted at the women's meeting went home and urged her husband to give himself to Christ, and he did so that night. Now she is going round to her neighbours' houses holding little meetings, and wonders at herself, for she was always timid and retiring. And so the good work spreads." From Charters Towers came a similar testimony, concluding as follows: " One of the converts called to see me this evening, a young man about thirty years of age. He has been in Australia for about ten years, and never entered a church until he came to one of your meetings, under the influence of drink. At that meeting he was utterly broken down, and went away the picture of misery. He came again and again, and sought and found salvation. It would be hard to describe the change in the man. He is indeed a new creature, 'transformed,' 'clothed, and in his right mind.' He asks me to write home and tell his father of the change he has experienced. His father is a class leader and chapel steward in the old country." This example will suffice of how the transforming work of the Spirit was made manifest. All the results can never be told. To tell all the story would be a monotonous repetition of crowded congregations, marvellous manifestations of Divine power, prayer answered, sinners converted, and believers quickened and blessed.

Our homeward journey commenced August 5th, when we left Townsville for Brisbane. A three days' sail within the Barrier Reef, where it is smooth and safe as a river, was most enjoyable. We passed some of the most magnificent scenery on the Australian coast—one vast archipelago of islands, some barren as desert, some clothed in lovely green, some covered with dwarf pines, and all fantastic and mountainous as those on the west coast of Scotland, but rugged and grander far.

Fellow-passengers pointed out to us the positions of the various places of interest. One told us of the mobs of wild horses which are found in the Burnett district, and called our attention to the following paragraph, which is clipped from the *Maryborough Chronicle*:—

"Since last Christmas two men have shot two thousand four hundred of these 'brumbies' on Knockbreak and Rawbella runs. They make a living by sending the skins and hair to the southern markets. Most of these wild horses are 'weedy' beasts, but some are splendid animals. It would, however, cost more than they are worth to accomplish the difficult feat of yarding them and breaking them in."

Kind friends met us in Brisbane, and supplied all our needs for the railway journey to Sydney, where we arrived after travelling thirty hours. There we packed our luggage and saw it safely on board the steamer, but we went overland to meet the steamer at Adelaide. By this means we were able to give several additional services to places we should otherwise have missed. A Sabbath was spent at Parramatta, with the result that at least forty decided to seek the Lord. Among many letters received as we were leaving Sydney, containing good wishes and prayers for our welfare, was one from the President of the New South Wales Conference.

"We are devoutly thankful," he writes, "for the exhibitions of the saving power of the gospel we have seen under your ministry, and for the uplifting of the religious experience and life of many who were previously converted. Your methods have been justified by their results. Your sound, practical commonsense way of presenting the claims of God will linger with us, not only as a memory but as a guide to many preachers in their pulpit ministrations; and your faith, and courage, and determination in pressing home your message, afford us no little clue in seeking to ascertain the secret of successful gospel preaching. No one will be more earnest than yourself in declaring, ' To God be all the glory.' "

Much that follows is of a too personal character to quote; but the assurance of a still more enthusiastic welcome if we will return for a second visit to their shores, we much appreciated. We shall be glad to do so if the " cloud " moves that way again.

Two days at Melbourne afforded opportunity for renewing friendships there, and for giving the converts a parting word. Mrs. Raven again ministered to our necessities with her accustomed generosity and kindly goodwill. The Sisters of the mission presented my wife with a travelling-case just as the train was about to leave the station, giving her no time to remonstrate, or even properly to express her thanks. We reached Adelaide on Saturday, August 17, and were heartily welcomed by quite a host of friends who had assembled to greet us in the Master's name. Successful services were held on the Sabbath; and on the Tuesday, August 20, we were invited to a farewell social gathering, when many kind words were spoken by ministers and laymen, after which we were presented with a handsome illuminated address, which read as follows:—

"DEAR SIR,—In the name of your very many friends in South Australia, we bid you 'Farewell.' We greatly rejoice, not only in the preservation of your health and that of Mrs. Cook since you landed in our midst nearly eighteen months ago, and for your safe journey throughout Australia, Tasmania, and New Zealand, but that, by the further blessing of God, the missions you came to conduct have been wonderfully successful. To you it has been graciously given to use, with perfect appropriateness, the words of the apostle: 'Now thanks be unto God, which always causeth us to triumph in Christ; and maketh manifest the savour of His knowledge by us in every place.' Our most earnest prayer is, that, by the Holy Ghost, your lifelong labours may yet be more manifestly owned of God in the ingathering of souls to Christ and the quickening of His Church. We deeply sympathise with Mrs. Cook in the double bereavement which she has sustained of father and mother during her absence from the homeland. God has thus seen fit to postpone, for a little while, the reunion lovingly anticipated, even until that day when the gathering shall be in the Father's House. Having learned that this is your birthday, we wish you most heartily 'Many happy returns.' And now we commend you, with Mrs. Cook, to the care of Almighty God, through whose grace, having been made perfect in His Son, we look to meet you again in the eternity beyond this present.—H. HENWOOD TEAGUE (President of the Conference), JAMES HASLAM."

At the close hundreds of loving hearts bade us God-speed, and shook our hands until they ached.

My last words were in acknowledgment of the kindness, forbearance, and goodwill which had been uniformly extended to us by our fellow-workers, and of the warm-hearted hospitality and genial welcome which had everywhere greeted us during our travels.

Our first home in South Australia, and our last before leaving the continent, was with Sir John and Lady Colton. As soon as we reached their threshold, we were assured that they would be glad to entertain us as long as we chose to stay; and all the time we were with them, their unwearied kindness and consideration revealed the same eager earnestness to provide the best hospitality that was possible. If we had been their nearest relatives they could not have treated us with more cordiality and generosity. Sir John has a splendid record. Under all circumstances he has maintained his integrity, and been true to Christ and his Church. When he was premier, on more than one occasion Cabinet meetings were adjourned that he might attend his class-meeting, and affairs of the State were never allowed to interfere with duties to God and religion. Lady Colton is quite worthy of such a husband, and a good example to all who occupy the higher positions of life.

Our Australian tour was now a thing of the past. For guidance, protection, and wonderful blessing our hearts were full of praise to God. During eighteen months we had travelled twenty-five thousand miles, and visited all the large towns of the seven colonies, without a single hitch in the arrangements. Nothing had been permitted to interfere with the work. We had perfect health, and strength had been given me to conduct five hundred and sixty services. The results will be revealed in eternity. We had large expectations, but they were more than realised. Figures are not always reliable, but without them it is difficult to discriminate between one work of God and another. The same indefinite phrases might be used of a hundred conversions as of a thousand. Nearly ten thousand persons passed through our enquiry-rooms. Enquirers are not always converts, we all know, but, on the other hand, many were converted who did not make profession in that way. We have every reason to believe that almost as many joined the various churches after our missions as were reported enquirers. The following will speak for itself: "Only twice in the history of the South Australian Wesleyan Conference has there been an equal increase of membership to that which is reported this year." This is from the official report the year succeeding our visit. Nothing could be more abhorrent to common sense than an egotistical display of numbers, but a judicious representation of facts is necessary to a right appreciation of what God has done. We have no thought but to magnify His grace and to stimulate the faith of His workers. When we weigh these facts, and take into account the widely-extending influence of such a work, may we not well exclaim, "What hath God wrought!"

Join us, dear readers, in songs of praise to Him who blessed us exceeding abundantly above all we asked or thought.

> "When the Lord brought back those that returned to Zion,
> We were like unto them that dream.
> Then was our mouth filled with laughter,
> And our tongue with singing.

Then said they among the nations,
The Lord hath done great things for them.
The Lord hath done great things for us;
Whereof we are glad.
They that sow in tears shall reap in joy.
Though he goeth on his way weeping, bearing forth the seed,
He shall come again with joy bringing his sheaves with him."

"Precisely, these four *alls* are the corner-stones of the historic Church of Christ. I venture to affirm that the sublimest and the most effective words known to human history are those in which these four colossal *alls* were proclaimed as the foundation of the Kingdom of the one God, Father, Son, and Holy Ghost, in the Christian Church. Where in the whole range of recorded thought have you anything possessing such scope and sublimity as these commands?—

"'*All* power is given unto Me, in heaven and on earth.

"'Go ye, *therefore*, and make disciples of *all* nations, baptizing them into the one name of the Father, the Son, and the Holy Ghost.

"'Teaching them to observe *all* things, whatsoever I have commanded you.

"'And, lo, I am with you at *all* times, even unto the end of the world.'—MATT. xxviii. 18-20.

"So closes the first Gospel, and well it may close here, for the seventh heaven has been reached in the height of outlook:—

"All power.
"All nations.
"All commands.
"All times.

"These four *alls* of Christ, from His supreme commission to His disciples, are the four corner-stones of the Church of Christ."—REV. JOSEPH COOK, D.D.

CHAPTER XII

CEYLON

Batticaloa—Kalmunai—Trincomalee—Colombo—Moratuwa—
Kandy—Kuruna—Galle

WHEN we left England it was our intention to include India in our tour; but after travelling thirty thousand miles, and preaching five hundred and sixty times in Australia, we thought it best to postpone our visit to that country.

For a vigorous mission in India we shall need strength that is not nearly exhausted. We were anxious, however, to test the possibilities of work such as ours in the East, so decided to call at Ceylon on the homeward journey and conduct a few missions as an experiment.

Our first mission was held at Batticaloa, on the east coast of the island, two hundred and eighty miles from Colombo, where the heathen abound, and Christians are few and far between. Not that our work as a Church has been a failure. It has been most successful, but, compared with the heathen, the Christians are a mere handful. What has been accomplished is worthy of mention. Eighty years have passed since William Ault was appointed, by the survivors of Dr. Coke, to evangelise this eastern province. Now we have three missionaries, ten native ministers, dozens of local preachers and leaders, and hundreds of vigorous Church members. Natives, first in rank, wealth, and education, belong to us, as well as the poorest classes, low caste lime-burners and *dhobies*. Among the first, in Asia, to call themselves Methodists, this Batticaloa church was first, also, to support its own Tamil pastor, and to found a home mission for the neighbouring villages. The first Asiatic university graduate who entered the Christian ministry went from this Circuit, and scores of others trained in their schools are now witnessing for Christ. A mission has been started among the aboriginal Veddah tribes, which has already yielded most encouraging firstfruits.

Our first pleasurable surprise, on arrival, was the substantial character of our church and school buildings; but greater far was the sight of the singing band returning from the bazaars, where they had been holding open-air services, and inviting Mohammedans and Sivites to come and hear the English evangelist. Mr. West, the energetic and greatly-beloved superintendent, led the procession, followed by at least fifty singing Christians of varied colour, all lustily, if not melodiously, screaming the praises of Jesus. It was an inspiring scene to watch the enthusiasm of these converted heathen in their effort to save others, such as would have done credit to any church at home. Tamils, with their triple band of white ashes on the forehead; Moormen, with the tall basket hat of their race; Burghers, who are half-castes between Dutch and natives; and quite a host of children follow the singers and take their seats in the church. Those

DISTRICT SYNOD, COLOMBO.

of high caste sit nearest the preacher, those of low caste nearest the door. Some must not enter the church at all; if they do, the high caste people who are not Christians will leave. These seem to know their place, and stand outside at the open windows.

The church was thronged, when we entered, with eager, enquiring, curious, and scornful souls. My interpreter, Rev. W. H. Walton, a native minister, took his stand at one end of the communion-table, while I stood at the other end. Mr. West presided at the organ. The singing was more harmonious than it had been in the street. My prayer was interpreted sentence by sentence, and seemed to produce a deep impression upon the audience. I had already gone through the sermon with the interpreter, so that he was quite prepared. He translated with wonderful fluency and rapidity. After a few sentences I felt there was between us that affinity which is so essential to success. God had evidently guided us in the choice of the medium through whom I should speak. Trained in a Sivite home, he was thoroughly familiar with heathen thought, and was able to adapt my message to native ideas and idioms. This is no easy task to a European, because even after he has got hold of the Tamil language, the great difficulty is to use it aright. Every word has its meaning, and that meaning often conveys the very opposite religious idea to that which is intended. But with such an interpreter I needed to have no apprehension. He had already sifted the terminology, and knew how to avoid misconception. As the address proceeded the Divine power increased, and profound silence reigned. The

Mohammedans listened particularly well, as I spoke of sin and its deserved penalty; but when I told them of the Incarnate God, and of His dying love, it was amazing how impassive they became. Some got up and walked out. No notice was taken of their departure, the others sat stolid and immovable as ever. Not a muscle of their faces moved, until I wondered whether they understood the truths of which I was speaking.

The service closed with an appeal for immediate decision for Christ, but none responded. This was somewhat disappointing after the expectations we had cherished. I felt sure, however, that we had not laboured in vain. Impressions had been made which must help the reaping later on. The people must realise more fully the great fact of personal guilt. Dormant consciences must be awakened by the Holy Spirit's application of Divine truth. To create this sense of sin I dealt with the sterner truths of the Word the following night, but did not invite seekers forward. "Those who are anxious for their soul's salvation may call at the mission-house, and I will instruct and help them there."

Did any respond? Yes, a young man, greatly concerned, sought and found the Saviour in Mr. West's study. He proved to be an old student of the Central School, who was convinced, when he left school twelve years ago, of the claims of Christ, but had gone back from baptism because of his widowed mother, who was greatly distressed lest, if he became a Christian, he would not perform the funeral rites. This led to his lapsing entirely into heathenism again. The genuineness of his conversion was evidenced by his coming forward the next evening to make public confession of Christ.

Nor did he come alone. That night half-a-score of penitents professed to realise God's pardoning mercy. Among them was a heathen who had come thirty miles to the meetings, and a grandniece of the chief Modliar, or headman of the province.

The work had now thoroughly commenced, and our hearts were full of praise. Interest grew until the church was far too small to accommodate those who wished to hear. All castes were represented among the seekers. The highest and lowest stood together at the communion-rail, confessing Christ.

Letters poured in from those who had difficulties, of which the following is a specimen :—" (1) What was I before I came into this world ? If I was nothing, why do I find an inequality in the position of mankind ? If I was something, why does not the Bible speak about it as well as about the world to come ? (2) Before I was created did not God know all things concerning me ? If so, is not His will to my life as cause to effect ? Then the pre-ordained, and only this, happens. (3) Except God, who and what is Eternal ? " Others asked why I did not attempt to establish the superiority of Christianity over other religions, and lecture on the evidences. My answer was that I had not come to attack other religions, but to preach Christianity. Christianity is its own evidence. It will do for men what no other religion offers to do. Other religions contain beautiful precepts, but men find it impossible to obey them. Christianity gives the power to do what it requires to be done. This is not a theory, it is our experience, etc.

The mission commenced on the Wednesday, but Sunday was the great day of the feast. The service for young people in the afternoon was pre-eminently a season of grace and delight. Nearly all from the English Training and Girls' Boarding Schools came forward to avow allegiance to Christ. Radiant faces, with tears yet undried, told of seeking and finding the joy of the Lord. How many realised forgiveness we cannot state, but fifty, at least, professed to receive definite blessing.

I had come from England with considerable prejudice against the educational policy of the mission-house. Money and time spent on our schools might be used to better advantage. This view I had long defended. But knowledge, gained by contact with the difficulties to be surmounted, has convinced me that the schools are invaluable, even from an evangelistic point of view. In these cultivated spots we find the ripened grain all ready for the reaper; and the fact that nearly ninety per cent. of our native Christians have passed through the schools, speaks for itself. The missionaries are as much devoted to God as the men at home are, and as well able to judge of the methods most likely to be successful. We must trust them.

On Sunday night we "let down the nets for a draught" again, and had another "take," which caused great gladness among our people. Seventeen young men, chiefly from Christian homes, knelt at the communion-rail to dedicate their lives to God. One was a village-school teacher who, while calling himself a Christian, had never previously realised God's forgiving love. The number of enquirers had now reached one hundred and twenty-three. A few came forward to seek a higher Christian life. The majority were baptized Tamils and Burghers, who had not been converted. About twenty were unbaptized heathen. This result, in five days, satisfied us that even in the East want of knowledge of the language is no insuperable difficulty to an evangelist, especially where he labours among a people prepared, as these were, for his message.

The next day we drove twenty-four miles to Kalmunai, where Mr. and Mrs. Weaver are labouring. Mr. West had generously offered two days out of the seven promised to Batticaloa, to this jungle station. At first we demurred to this alteration in our programme: but when we learned how emphatically it meant helping those who needed us most we were glad to consent. The place abounds with snakes and all sorts of creeping things. Wild elephants and other dangerous animals are found within a few miles; but these are not worth the name of difficulties to the missionaries.

We found the work of God in a most prosperous condition. I reasoned during three-quarters of an hour "of righteousness, temperance, and judgment to come." The response was so ready and general that in a few minutes the vestries were filled. Next night witnessed a similar scene. Altogether eighty passed through the enquiry-rooms. Thirty were girls from the boarding-school, twenty-five were baptized Tamils, ten were Burghers, seventeen were heathen. Among them were four men from a village in the jungle thirty miles away, who had come to seek the light. Four others were very dark heathen, but had had some instruction from the catechist. A Sivite woman was converted, who had married a Christian teacher. The husband had become a backslider when he married her. Recently he had come back to Christ, but she had been his difficulty.

Returning to Batticaloa, we found our steamer would not sail until Saturday, which afforded opportunity for two additional services. Of the conversions we rejoiced over, none was more important than the case of the "vanniah," a native government official of high rank, who had been a Christian some years ago, but had married a heathen wife and lapsed into formalism, in which he was more a heathen than a Christian. But most interesting were two "raw heathen," or the nearest approach to that we have to report. Both said they had never heard the gospel before, except at the open-air and bazaar services. Whether or not they are genuine cases of conversion, only time will prove, but the fact that we had only two such cases is instructive. All the others had been, more or less, under Christian teaching, which makes the lesson plain that the prospects of conversion, when the day of revival comes, will be proportionate to the amount of steady preparation which has preceded the visit of the evangelist. Much such preparatory work has been done, and there are openings everywhere for the reaper.

Trincomalee, our next place of labour, is a naval station, as well as a heathen centre. Our week there was, consequently, divided between European and native services. This did not facilitate success. The concentration so essential in mission work could not be maintained. Better results would have followed,

I believe, had I devoted the whole time to the natives. As it was, we have no reason to complain of the results, but the division of labour was a source of weakness. Between seventy and eighty professed conversion, among them several soldiers and a sailor. A service for educated natives produced a deep impression. Those who had difficulties, and desired help, were invited to call at the mission-house the following day. Three men responded, who wished to know more perfectly concerning the way of life. One was a Sivite preacher, who had not long returned from a religious pilgrimage to India, in connection with which he had hoped to find rest to his soul. But he came back more dissatisfied than ever. His confidence in heathenism was shaken when he saw the fanaticism of the people, and how the Brahmins traded upon their superstitions. Through reading his Bible, and attending our church occasionally, he had since become convinced of the Divinity and claims of Christ. But to confess Him meant breaking with all his friends, persecution, and opposition in his home, and irreparable financial loss. The mission, however, furnished the necessary impetus, and I had the joy of baptizing him before I left. It was beautiful to see his face as he confessed his faith in the risen Christ. This one case was worth all our effort.

During our visit to Trincomalee, we witnessed a scene which stirred our hearts to their depth. In a heathen procession was a man with his lips and tongue fastened together with a skewer, and the flesh and muscles of his back pierced with iron hooks. To these were attached ropes, by which he was driven as though he were a horse. It was a sickening sight;

but the man appeared contented enough, and seemed even to take a savage delight in the torture he was enduring. Such voluntary suffering brings merit which secures certain blessedness in the world to come. This is what they are taught, and there is no difficulty in finding victims when they are needed. We felt it to be a great privilege to be sent with the lamp of life to these benighted souls.

Our overland journey from Trincomalee to Colombo afforded opportunity of seeing the forest country, which otherwise we should have missed. We travelled in a bullock-waggon through the jungle, where wild beasts are still occasionally seen. As there were no seats in the waggon, we sat at the back until darkness set in, when we reclined on straw at the bottom. The jolting of the cart, the tinkling of the bells round the bullocks' necks, and the loud blasts of the horn rendered sleep impossible. This, combined with the strange surroundings, made us the more thankful when morning dawned. Twenty-four hours of such travelling was quite enough: but what we saw amply compensated for the inconvenience we suffered. To a lover of Nature the journey from Kandy to Colombo is the greatest possible treat. We passed through long stretches of tea, cocoa, and coffee plantations, placed amidst enchanting mountain scenery, with rivers, waterfalls, and ravines, the grandeur of which nothing could exceed. Rice fields were strangely interspersed with belts of jungle, the vivid light green of the one contrasting in a wonderful way with the darker colouring of the other. That travellers should regard this journey as one of the most varied and interesting in the world we do not at all wonder. It

CEYLONESE FERNS.

has well been described as "one of the show-places of the universe." The same is true of Ceylon as a whole.

Its names—"Lanka, the resplendent," of the Brahmins; "the pearl drop on the brow of India," of the Buddhists; "the island of the jewels," of the Chinese; "the land of the hyacinth and ruby," of the Greeks; and "the home of Adam and Eve," according to the Mohammedans—will show the high esteem in which the island has been held by various nations; for beauty of vegetation and scenery and interest attaching to its people, towns, and ancient monuments, Ceylon is unsurpassed by any land in the universe.

Our Colombo mission was held in the Pettah Church, one of the oldest Protestant places of worship in Asia. It is situated near to Wesley College, and its congregation consists largely of educated persons. No need for an interpreter there; all speak or understand English, which was a great relief to the missioner. Attending the college are over five hundred youths, including Buddhists, Hindus, Mohammedans, and those of several other religions. From these chiefly we gathered our converts. Some came from Colpetty School, and others were Burghers and Europeans, but the majority were youths who had been trained at Wesley. To Rev. J. Passmore much credit is due for the efficiency and high reputation of this institution. The scholastic results had been such that many heathen parents prefer ours to the Government college, where strict religious neutrality is maintained. That much has been done also in inculcating Christian principles and developing Christian character is evident from the preparedness I found among the young men to decide for Christ. Many were quite ready for the opportunity the mission afforded to make public dedication of their lives to God. During six days we took the names of one hundred and thirty-eight persons who came forward as seekers of salvation. Among the seekers were twelve sons of native ministers and several who are preparing for the various professions. One was son of the chief Modliar, or headman of the Kandy province, who will probably take his father's place. All sorts and conditions came to Jesus and bore testimony to His preciousness. Surely this universal adaptibility of the gospel is proof sufficient of its Divine origin.

The people among whom we laboured were chiefly Sinhalese, Tamils, and Burghers. The Tamils are chiefly found on the eastern portion of the island, and comprised the majority of our hearers at Batticaloa, Kalmunai, and Trincomalee. Burghers predominated, with a sprinkling of educated natives, at Kandy, Galle, and Colombo. At Kuruna and Moratuwa our congregations consisted almost entirely of Sinhalese. God has done a work through Methodism at these two places which ranks among the greatest triumphs of missions.

Situated in the very heart of Buddhism, Moratuwa, with its twenty thousand inhabitants, possesses more real Christians than many a town in England the same size can claim. In the town itself, besides what other churches report, we have six hundred church members, and between two and three thousand adherents. It was a stirring sight to see the church crowded, each night during our mission, with six to eight hundred people, all eager and anxious for the Word of Life.

The rainy season had set in, but, notwithstanding heavy tropical showers at service time, the people came. Except that the congregation was dark-skinned and dressed differently, it was just such an one as we should have had in England. All were reverent, well-dressed, familiar with our hymns and tunes, and hearty, as Methodists should be. It was almost too much like home. Their responses during prayer, and their sparkling eyes and shouts of praise when sinners came to the communion-rail, seemed more like Yorkshire than Ceylon. Speaking through an interpreter did not at all interfere with the effectiveness of the service. My interpreters forgot themselves in their work, and the union of two heads and two hearts seemed to increase the effect rather than diminish it. The liberty and power we had was wonderful. I preached the same sort of sermon I should have preached to an English audience, and was pleased to find the more thoughtful addresses were most appreciated. Before going to the East I had no idea that we had achieved such successes in the establishment of native churches. Such vigorous religious life and attachment to Methodist doctrines and polity in Ceylon came to me as a pleasant surprise. Sinners came forward at every service, broken down and penitent, until one hundred and sixty had professed to receive remission of sins. This result, in five days, prophesied of great possibilities had we been able to remain longer. The enquirers belonged, chiefly, to Christian families; some were of the second and third generation of Christians, sons and daughters of our own people.

Kuruna has a history not unlike Moratuwa. Under the direction of the Rev. Spence Hardy, a native minister laboured there with signal success, forming a church among a heathen community such as will compare favourably with our English churches. During our visit we were rather embarrassed, at first, by a new interpreter; but he soon adapted himself and proved a capital medium, as all the native ministers did. In four days seventy persons professed decision for Christ. The number of men among the seekers was a most pleasing feature.

Kandy and Galle were the last two places on our list. Kandy has a population of twenty-three thousand, and is uniquely beautiful. It is surrounded by hills and set, gem-like, in an amphitheatre. Travellers describe it as one of the most charming towns in the world, and certainly we saw nothing to compare with it. Kandy ranks among the most sacred of Buddhist towns, because it possesses the temple which contains the so-called relic of Buddha's tooth, to which kings and priests of Burmah, Siam, and China send offerings, and come on pilgrimage at various times.

Our work at Kandy, as already mentioned, was among English-speaking people. The weather interfered with our congregations the first few nights, but interest increased until the church was filled at each service. Those of other churches worked with us, particularly the agents of the Church Missionary Society, and all churches shared in the benefit. We heard much of the mission conducted by Rev. George C. Grubb a few years ago, and found precious fruit remaining. Several tea-planters who were converted at that time are now earnest workers for Christ. More than a hundred seekers were helped in the enquiry-rooms during our visit, and Christians were quickened and blessed. After we left, the Rev. E. A. Prince wrote as follows:—" The life of the whole Church beats with a stronger and warmer pulse. All the classes have received additions, and are more encouraging than before. On Sunday evening I had the pleasure of welcoming thirteen persons to the Lord's Supper for the first time—three of these were English soldiers. . . . Another soldier was converted the week following." Our reply to Mr. Prince's complaint that we did not stay long enough was to the effect that we were only there to test the possibilities of work like ours. Our next visit will not be to experiment, but to conduct a prolonged mission as we should do in England.

Passing through Colombo on our way to Galle, I held a service at the Wellawatta Industrial School, where one hundred and twenty youths were being educated and trained to work. Because both Tamils and Sinhalese were present, I was obliged to have two interpreters—one for each language. It was rather slow work, but we soon forgot the difficulties in the great purpose of the service, and God was pleased to abundantly bless our labour. That night eighteen lads gave satisfactory evidence of intelligent trust in Christ. Afterwards I examined these one by one, and others who had recently confessed Christ, and was so well satisfied with their genuineness that we resolved to admit twenty to baptism without delay. On the night before we left Ceylon, it was my joy to perform the ceremony, and to receive them publicly into the Church of Christ. It was decided that the others should be baptized after a more lengthened period of probation. Most were from Sivite and Buddhist homes, but one was a Moor, of which race not half a dozen have been converted since our missions in Ceylon commenced.

In the Galle district our Church's work has been chiefly educational, which prepares the way of the Lord much more than those can realise who have not visited these eastern countries. A great harvest is ripening there for the reaper, as will appear from the results we witnessed the few days we spent at that station. Of the eighty-five enquirers reported, most were from the schools, and thirty belonged to heathen families.

None rejoiced more over the success of our work than the missionaries. Their thankfulness for the help we were able to render in gathering in the harvest for which they had laboured, was as gratifying as it was stimulating. The fact should be recognised that all missionaries are not reapers, any more than all ministers in English Circuits are. Some who are endowed richly with other gifts do not possess that peculiar suasive influence which is such an important factor in bringing souls to immediate decision for Christ. One sows and another reaps. New faces and presentations of truth, to say nothing of new methods, create fresh interest, and win some who would never be won by those with whose ministry they have become familiar. Periodical visits from evangelists are almost more necessary to the mission-fields than they are to the home Circuits. Thousands of young people from heathen homes are receiving instruction in our schools. If these pass through our hands without conversion, it is almost certain that the great majority will lapse again into heathenism. Most of the educated heathen with whom I have conversed were educated in mission-schools, and are now the more formidable opponents of Christianity because of the education we have given them. To allow these to go from us without Christ, is nothing short of a calamity. Those on the spot will be successful with some, but strangers are required to influence others. It is our profound conviction that hundreds have been lost to Christ and Methodism who would have been easily won had evangelists been sent out from time to time to assist the missionaries.

The fact that, during the two months of our visit, nearly nine hundred persons professed to realise God's forgiving love in our services, will speak for itself of the possibilities to an evangelist if a lengthened tour could be arranged.

Among the educated natives were some of the most promising cases. And it is a point to be noted that when I preached through an interpreter we had almost invariably larger visible results than when I preached without an interpreter. The missionaries thought that the impetus our visit gave to the spiritual life of our churches will be among the best and farthest reaching results. Not less important, in our view, was the educating of native ministers to do similar work. To inspire and encourage these was our constant aim. Nothing impressed us more than the ability and zeal of those who acted as our interpreters. Untold possibilities are before them with a little more faith in God and themselves. Some caught the flame, and carried on the work after we left. One tells of twenty-six converts the following week. Another sends a parting letter, in which he says: "Not only our people, but we preachers also, have been blessed. Your message, and the results which followed its delivery, have intensified and deepened our faith in the Atonement of our Lord Jesus Christ, and have inspired us with fresh zeal for His service. We shall be more effective preachers—because more consecrated—and more faithful stewards of the mysteries of the Gospel for having heard you. . . . I have already taken occasion to refer, in the public congregation, to the good I have received, and the lessons I have learned by attending your missions. . . ."

What the native Christians thought of our visit will appear from the following address which was presented to us when we left Batticaloa. It was signed by more than two hundred persons, all natives except about twelve:—

"DEAR MR. COOK,—We desire in this, the last, service of your mission in Batticaloa, to express to you our deep sense of gratitude for the blessing which, both as individuals and as a church, we have, by God's grace, received in connection with your visit to us.

"We thank you for the unsparing devotion with which you have laboured, and for the patience and kindness with which, in spite of exhausting heat and the embarrassments of interpretation, you have sought to help us.

"Our praise is given to God for the blessing we have received, but you have been the minister of God unto us for good.

"The Word you have preached has been a living Word; old truths have shone with new light and beauty as you have set them before us; and under your clear and forceful preaching many of us have been led into a richer and fuller enjoyment of the Christian life; our young men have been made bold to confess Christ their Saviour, and more fully to consecrate their lives to Him; numbers of our children have been led to Jesus; and souls of all ages have found, through faith in Him, the joy of a present salvation. We believe, moreover, that many of the heathen who have listened in such numbers to you from evening to evening have been deeply impressed with the truth, and that further fruit to your labour will appear in later days.

"Your visit will be a precious memory to our church, and your name will live in our homes and in our hearts. We earnestly and affectionately invite you to visit us again, if the way be made clear for your return to the East; and we hope that then once more we shall have the pleasure of welcoming Mrs. Cook, whose presence with you on this arduous mission tour has been an added joy to us all, and an encouragement to Christian enterprise to all the ladies of our church.

"We beg you to be the bearer of our very grateful thanks to the Home Mission Committee, the Foreign Missionary Committee, and to the Conference, for permitting you to undertake this mission, and to be yourself the mediator of our request to them, that at an early date you may once more be commissioned to make a prolonged visit to our Ceylon and Indian mission-fields."

But for the hearty co-operation of the missionaries, the result we rejoiced over would not have been possible. Most gratefully do I acknowledge their uniform courtesy, sympathy, and goodwill. To Rev. T. Mosscrop, the indefatigable chairman of the Colombo district, we were particularly indebted. The efficiency and completeness of his arrangements greatly facilitated the success.

Our service has not been without blemishes and defects, but God has been pleased so richly to bless it that praise shall be our prevailing note. He alone giveth the increase. And the victories of the past are but a pledge and earnest of other victories, grander and more glorious. A dying Buddhist priest said to one of our people who visited him: "Christianity is like the sun rising in the morning. Already its light is seen above the tops of the mountains, and it will rise higher and higher until its light is everywhere. Buddhism and other religions are like the setting sun; they are sinking lower and lower, as the sun sinks in the west." That testimony is true. All other lights shall wane before the presence of Him who is the Light of the world. The day shall come which shall be signalised by His universal triumph. We may not see it before "this mortal shall have put on immortality," but we appreciate the privilege of being permitted to assist in hastening that glorious era.

"O that men would praise the Lord for His goodness, and for His wonderful works to the children of men. . . ." "What shall I render unto the Lord for all His benefits toward me! . . ." "I will offer to Thee the sacrifice of thanksgiving." These words exactly express our feeling as we look back upon the way in which we were led. Now that we are at home again, and have time to quietly review our tour, we are better able to realise how wonderfully we were helped and blessed. God hath indeed dealt bountifully with us. Of one thing we are perfectly satisfied that the old gospel has lost none of its power. Whatever else has changed in this nineteenth century, the gospel, preached in the power of the Holy Spirit, is the same power it ever was. Rightly experienced, lived, and preached, it will produce the same results as followed its declaration in olden times. We have seen all classes and creeds bow before its force, and have had our lifelong conviction intensified that the old-fashioned reliance upon God and on the power of the gospel is all that is needed to save men to-day, as it was in the early days of Christianity. There is no new method of bringing men to God — the Church must return to first principles.

So closes our story of two years of grace. To God and the Lamb be praise for ever!

"The banner under which we serve can never know defeat,
And so we'll lay our laurels down at our great Captain's feet."

www.ingramcontent.com/pod-product-compliance
Lightning Source LLC
Chambersburg PA
CBHW030011240426
43672CB00007B/913